1994

THE OFFICIAL BOOK OF
THE NEW YORK RANGERS
STANLEY CUP CHAMPIONSHIP

by Stu Hackel
Introduction by John Davidson
Photography by Bruce Bennett Studios

NEW YORK RANGERS

The 1994 Stanley Cup Champion New York Rangers.

Front row, left to right: *Mike Richter, Kevin Lowe, Steve Larmer, Dick Todd - Assistant Coach, Neil Smith - President and General Manager, Mark Messier - Captain, Mike Keenan - Head Coach, Colin Campbell - Associate Coach, Brian Leetch, Adam Graves, Glenn Healy.* Second row: *Mike Folga - Trainer, Joe Murphy - Trainer, Glenn Anderson, Joe Kocur, Alexei Kovalev, Craig MacTavish, Sergei Nemchinov, Sergei Zubov, Dave Smith - Trainer, Bruce Lifrieri, Trainer.* Third row: *Esa Tikkanen, Greg Gilbert, Jay Wells, Stephane Matteau, Jeff Beukeboom, Doug Lidster, Brian Noonan.* Fourth row: *Mike Hartman, Mike Hudson, Alexander Karpovtsev, Ed Olczyk, Nick Kypreos.*

1994 – The Official Book of the New York Rangers Stanley Cup Championship © 1994 by the New York Rangers.

All rights reserved. The use of any part of this publication reproduced, transmitted in any form or by any means, electronic, mechanical, photocopying, recording, or otherwise or stored in a retrieval system, without the prior written consent of the publisher is an infringement of copyright law.

This book is an official publication of the New York Rangers. Production Director: Kevin Kennedy; Executive Editor: Barry Watkins; Associate Editors: Kevin McDonald and John Rosasco; Editorial Assistants: Ann Marie Gilmartin, Rob Koch, and Karin Strelec. Special thanks to Stu Hackel, whose dedication and tireless effort made this publication possible.

Thanks to: The photographers at Bruce Bennett Studios, including Bruce Bennett, John Giamundo, Jim Leary, Scott Levy, Jim McIsaac, and Brian Winkler; Rene Vargas for designing and programming the Madison Square Garden marquee; Mike McCarthy, Joe Whelan and the Madison Square Garden Network production department, and the New Jersey Devils and SportsChannel for use of game-action video.

New York Rangers Stanley Cup cover image renderd by Mary Cummings.

New York Times photo, page 96.

About the author: Stu Hackel is a native New Yorker who spent nine years at the NHL where he was director of broadcasting, publishing, and video. His writing on hockey has appeared in Sports Illustrated, The Hockey News, Goal Magazine, and The Village Voice as well as in numerous NHL books and publications.

Printed in the United States of America by Applied Graphics Technologies, Fleetwood Graphics Division, Moonachie, New Jersey.

Video capture: Symbols, The Art of Communication, Toronto, Ontario.

Film: Moveable Type, Toronto, Ontario.

Editing, design, production: Dan Diamond and Associates, Toronto, Ontario.

1994

NEW YORK RANGERS

THE OFFICIAL BOOK OF THE NEW YORK RANGERS
STANLEY CUP CHAMPIONSHIP
Contents

Mark Messier's second period goal proved to be the Stanley Cup-winner in Game Seven against the Vancouver Canucks.

OH BABY!
WHAT A YEAR

by John Davidson

IF YOU'RE A WINNER IN NEW YORK, you're a winner forever. Win in New York and you become part of New York folklore, not just part of sports history. Your victory never dies. And now that the Rangers are the 1994 Stanley Cup Champions – this city will never let these guys forget it.

This Stanley Cup proves the greatness of Mark Messier. It proves that Michael Keenan can win the Stanley Cup. It proves that Neil Smith made the right moves. It proves that the organization above the Rangers, through their cooperation, their ability to hire good people, their ability to listen to good people, and their professional approach, made a lot of correct decisions. And the players proved that a hockey team can win in New York. They have finally defeated the past.

The past had always haunted the Rangers. It was brought up by kids, adults, opposition fans, Ranger fans, and the media. It was a favorite way to mock the hockey club. In previous years, the very thought of "*1940*" would send shudders through the team. But this year's Rangers took "*1940*," looked at the "*94*" in the middle and gassed the "*1*" and the "*0*."

When a Ranger team does well, new fans are born throughout the region. People still tell me the 1979 team I played for turned them into Ranger fans. Now, a whole new generation of fans has been born in 1994. These fans are of all different ages, too. It could be a woman who had only watched three games in her life. It could be a newborn, whose parents will always identify its birth with the time the Rangers won the Stanley Cup. It could be

MSG Network's John Davidson starred for the Rangers in the 1979 Stanley Cup playoffs.

kids who are looking to connect with a new sport and are thrilled by the Rangers' championship.

Not long ago, I went to a school program for my seven-year-old daughter Ashley. There were ten boys in the program, and eight of them told me that their favorite sport was hockey. That reaction is incredible for this area and the Rangers' success is the main reason why.

You couldn't even imagine saying this just over a year ago. After 1993, no one knew what to expect this year. There had been great turmoil. But Mike Keenan's hiring seemed to solidify the team. Mike grabbed hold early and all the turmoil disappeared. There was instant focus on the upcoming season, a focus that quickly took hold and took shape with the two wins in England over Toronto last September. Everyone was on the same page.

A big contributing factor to the new attitude was when Keenan asked MSG Network to assemble a video tape of the Mets ticker-tape victory parade in 1986. It was created by Joe Whelan, my producer at the Network, and Mike showed it to the players on the first day of training camp. The tape was so well done, it made the players crave a playoff championship of their own. For some of the younger players and some of the veterans not familiar with New York, the video showed how captivating it can be when you do well in this city. With this image of success firmly in mind, everyone began to concentrate on their common long-term goal – winning the Stanley Cup.

THE TEAM BEGAN THE SEASON TRYING TO FIND ITSELF, BUT SOON BECAME A CONSISTENT FAVORITE IN EACH GAME.

THE RANGERS PLAYED MORE than 110 games, and led the League for almost the entire season. This team had to learn how to handle success, something very difficult to do. They played any number of big games in the course of the season and won every one of them. They won in different ways: on the road, at home, playing defense, scoring in bunches, getting hot goaltending, hitting, and scoring late goals.

Because of leadership, the 1993-94 Rangers competed every night. Mark Messier says he learned about competing from his father and from Wayne Gretzky, and this team learned from Messier and Keenan. Early in the season, Keenan challenged the team and individuals to improve on their deficiencies, and the players accepted it. When you see the kind of complete player Brian Leetch has become, it's because he accepted Mike's challenge.

This team also had the ability to improve while they were winning. In many other organizations, management would not take those types of chances. But Neil Smith and the Rangers management made big changes while the club was in first place overall. They understood that these changes were necessary to win in the playoffs.

So, examining all these factors, it's not an exaggeration to say the 1994 Rangers are truly a great team.

Of course, what really makes a team great is how it performs in the playoffs. Previous Ranger teams tended to reflect the character of the city — they were either very high or very low. There was very little middle ground. For a hockey team, that's a character flaw. This team battled against that. They remained very focused and had no fear of adversity. This helped them become a successful playoff team.

Many people ask me to compare this team to the 1978-79 Rangers. We had a substantial team, with players of some character like Phil Esposito,

Carol Vadnais, and Anders Hedberg. All were exceptional playoff performers. We had a good regular season and, obviously, we did well in the playoffs. But we didn't come close to matching the depth of the talent on this team. We were the classic playoff underdogs who played loose with nothing to lose. So there's really no comparison.

WHEN YOU PLAY IN THE FINALS FOR THE FIRST TIME, YOU ONLY REALIZE WHAT IT MEANS AFTER IT'S OVER.

WHEN THE PLAYOFFS BEGIN, you try to put yourself into a focused cocoon, to stay away from outside influences and distractions so you can play your best. You get into a routine and if things go well, you stick with it: your stretching, your superstitions, your pre-game meal, your amount of warm-up time, your complete game-day preparation, your night before the game. You get into habits and repetition, you maintain the same emotional level, the same standards of behavior, because they're working.

If you change, you risk second-guessing yourself and if doubt creeps in, it can damage your ability to play instinctively. You need your instincts to play at your best. In the playoffs, when you're in good shape and mentally strong, if your instincts are good, you are a complete package ready for what you hope will be a two-month grind. You may have to play 28 games in 56 nights. You may have to play injured and you can have no fear of losing.

When you compare notes with athletes from other sports, the playoff grind is what they find most remarkable about NHL hockey. Winning a championship in any sport is an ordeal, but I defy anyone to tell me there's a tougher championship to win than the Stanley Cup. The Stanley Cup Finals are a fascinating experience, the best two weeks of your life. But you don't realize this until later.

In the playoffs when fans are at an emotional peak, the only people who are calm are the players. It's critical that you contain your emotions —

especially in the biggest games. One crazy mistake can cost a team the series and the season. I think it's easier to deal with the whole structure – the preparation, the meaning, and the pressure of the Finals – if you've been there before. That's why the veterans on the 1994 Rangers were so crucial to the club's success.

THE PLAYOFFS ARE THE SEASON OF THE GOALIE

DURING THE REGULAR SEASON, hockey is great entertainment and the fans come out to see great goal scorers do their thing. If Vancouver's in town, they come to watch Pavel Bure. If Pittsburgh's here, they come to see Mario Lemieux. But in the playoffs, the goalies reign. It doesn't matter how good Pavel Bure is, because if Kirk McLean doesn't play well, the Canucks don't make the Finals. As good as Mark Messier, Alexei Kovalev and even Brian Leetch are, it is Mike Richter who gives the Rangers a chance to win.

The biggest pressure you face as a goaltender is to get yourself in a groove of playing well at the very start of the playoffs. The playoffs aren't difficult if you start well. Your sole job in the playoffs is to concentrate, work hard, and stop the puck for two months. Frankly, if you get off to a good start in the playoffs, you'll immediately be recognized for it, your team will do well, your confidence level will go sky-high, and away you go!

But if you start the playoffs slowly, it's a real struggle. Then the goaltender faces life and death: a must-win in every game. Your team is in a hole and the heat is squarely on you.

We certainly started well in 1979 and got on a roll. When we beat the Islanders in the Semi-Finals, for the first time since I had become a Ranger, the team captured the hearts of New Yorkers. But then we ran into the Canadiens in the Finals. They had won the Cup three years in a row, whereas a lot of us had never been this far before. When that big Montreal machine started to roll, there was no stopping them. And when we lost, it was horrible. It's true we were beaten by a great team and that a lot of people respected the fact that we got that far. We were gratified to have reached the final round of the playoffs, but we still didn't win. It's something all of us on that team have had to live with.

But now, for our team, 1979 is dead. And all the ghosts that have haunted this team before and since are dead. Long live 1994!

I'm from Calgary but I live here now. As a player and broadcaster, I've been identified with the Rangers for almost two decades, and during that time, the organization has been terrific to me. But sports franchises have their ups and downs and you have to go through both the good and the bad. And when the Rangers have struggled, New Yorkers can be pretty vocal – whether they are Ranger fans or not. I've certainly heard a lot over the years. But now that the Rangers are finally the Stanley Cup Champions, even though I'm a little farther from the ice than I was when I played, I'm still very, very proud to be a part of it. It makes me want to light up a cigar and puff my chest up a little bit.

From all the former Rangers, to the Rangers of 1994, thank you!

Mike Richter's four shutouts in the 1994 playoffs tied the NHL record for most shutouts in one playoff year. **7**

Heave Ho! Ranger Dreams on Parade

by Stu Hackel

IT STARTED AT THE END — WITH A PARADE. Not a real parade, but the notion of a parade, the video image of a parade coach Mike Keenan showed to the players on the first day of training camp. It planted a dream in their minds. But for that dream to come true, there was much work to do. Dreams don't fall from the sky like confetti and ticker-tape. Dreams defy the laws of gravity. You've got to go get them, tie a rope around them and give a mighty "heave-ho" to pull dreams from the clouds to earth.

It had always been the same story. For 54 years, through more than 4,000 games and 600 different players, someone else's dream came true. Another team always won the Stanley Cup. Another team skated off with it, drank champagne from it, took it to the parade. Just once, why couldn't the Rangers win the Cup? Just once.

The 1993-94 Rangers were going to have a dream season. They'd set franchise records of all sorts — records for wins, points, road victories, and shorthanded goals. They would have long unbeaten streaks and avoid prolonged slumps. They would have the best power play in the league and one of the best penalty killing records. The franchise would host the NHL All-Star Game and have four of its players on the Eastern Conference roster. Their goaltender would be named the All-Star Game's

MVP. They would have nine 20-goal scorers, another new club record. One of their players would set a team record for most goals. They would break their five-year victory drought on Long Island. They would finish first in their division, first in their conference and first overall in the league during the regular season. They would win the Conference Championship in the playoffs. That would be enough for most teams – but not the 1993-94 New York Rangers. They wanted the Stanley Cup and they wanted the parade that goes with it.

It didn't seem like a dream season at first. Mike Richter was winless. Several players were benched. Jeff Beukeboom was a holdout. Sergei Zubov was in such poor condition, he was scratched from the lineup and even sent to the minors for a game. Twice the Rangers had to come from behind to beat weak teams. And then, on October 19, they lost to the Anaheim Mighty Ducks, a new franchise playing just the sixth game in its history.

Fifteen minutes into a lackluster practice on October 21, Keenan celebrated his forty-fourth birthday by smashing his stick over a goal, flinging the shaft over the glass and ordering the players off the ice and into the dressing room. A ten-minute meeting followed in which Keenan not-so-politely reminded the players of the commitment they had made to hard work and winning before the season began. "The message got across," said Kevin Lowe.

Adam Graves in the victorious Ranger dressing room.

They lost again the next night in Tampa Bay. Captain Mark Messier called it the "worst game we've played all year," but Keenan, somehow, saw some signs of improvement. No one was sure what he was talking about.

A pair of games followed against the teams that had played for the Stanley Cup in 1993. A third-period goal from Esa Tikkanen defeated the Kings. For Mike Richter, this first victory brought psychological relief, justifying the coach's faith in his abilities. Later in the week, on October 28, the Stanley Cup champion Montreal Canadiens came to town, and in one very exciting game, the Rangers grabbed a tie on Adam Graves' tip-in with ten seconds remaining. The Rangers were now undefeated in two.

When the Canadiens returned to the Garden 11 games and 26 days later, the Rangers still had not lost. Neither had Richter, who was playing with confidence and elan. They beat the Canadiens that night and Ottawa the next for their 14th consecutive game without a defeat. They went 11-1-1 in November, tying the club mark for best record in a month. Graves was piling up goals while Tikkanen piled up points. Sergei Nemchinov was getting key points while checking the opposition's top players. Young Alexei Kovalev displayed flashes of brilliance. Lowe, shaking off injury, played with great consistency. The power play had become lethal, as Zubov rounded into shape. Brian Leetch, challenged by Keenan to concentrate on his defensive play, had begun to make good on his promise. And Messier was Messier. It was not only a better team, it was also becoming a different team. President and general manager Neil Smith worked diligently to reach satisfactory terms with Beukeboom. He also engineered a three-way deal with Hartford and Chicago, getting one of hockey's most underrated stars in Steve Larmer and a rugged role player in Nick Kypreos.

They lost on the Island on November 27, then went undefeated for another seven games. Beginning with their October 24 win over Los Angeles until a December 29 victory in St. Louis, the Rangers won 21 games, lost three and tied

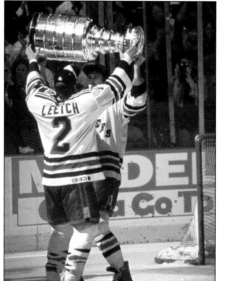

Kevin Lowe passes the Cup to playoff MVP Brian Leetch.

three. They were the NHL's "Best in Show," playing with speed, skill and finesse. Their goaltending, defense, and special teams led the League. They worked hard during games and just as hard between them. They rode stationary bikes as if they were in training for the six-day bicycle races at the old Garden in the 1930s. Those who rarely played, "The Black Aces," showed dedication equal to that of the regulars. Before the start of each practice, after the players had stretched, the regulars and the Aces shouted in unison, "Heave-ho! Heave-ho! Heave-ho!" pulling the rope tied to the dream, pulling the dream closer.

Still, Smith and Keenan recognized gaps in the Rangers' play that, come the stretch drive and playoff time, might turn 54 years into 55. As spring approached, other talented clubs began to emerge. The New Jersey Devils, always in the rear-view mirror, now pulled up alongside as Rangers slowed down, playing .500 hockey in February and March. Then Neil Smith put the pedal to the metal. On March 21, he dealt Mike Gartner and Tony Amonte as part of three deals that returned Glenn Anderson, Craig MacTavish, Stephane Matteau, and Brian Noonan. "I knew these wouldn't be popular trades," said Smith, but he also knew he had acquired needed size and experience in four tough players who had all been to the Finals, and two who had been champions.

Heave-ho. With eight new hands to pull on the rope, over the last dozen games the Rangers won eight and tied two. The new quartet made an immediate impact. Richter set new personal and team records for victories. The defensemen and forwards all began to bang bodies. When suspensions and injury depleted the ranks at center, Keenan temporarily moved Kovalev into the middle where he emerged as a dynamic force. The power play soared with Zubov and Leetch at the controls. Larmer seemed to contribute everywhere. And, of course, Messier was Messier. Graves passed Vic Hadfield's Ranger record of 50 goals in a season. He was handed the puck for number 51 and said "I wish I could cut it up into 25 pieces and give one to each of my teammates." It was quintessential Graves and typical of the Rangers' unity as they held off the Devils and were crowned regular-season champions.

And then, the playoffs — the biggest "heave-ho" of all — the most compelling two months of hockey New York has ever seen. With each game, with each passing round, the City, the suburbs, and the sticks were increasingly drawn to the unfolding story of the hockey club. By June 14, the entire region would be mesmerized. Long-time fans, recounting their years of suffering, were now celebrated in their own neighborhoods and in the media. Innumerable new fans

Nick Kypreos shares the Rangers' moment of triumph.

jumped on the first Rangers bandwagon in memory. And why not? Cynics say everybody loves a winner, but this was different — this was the eternal loser coming out on top.

IN THE RANGERS, PEOPLE WHO KNEW NOTHING ABOUT HOCKEY SAW A CHILD'S FAIRY TALE COMING TO LIFE.

They saw the frog turning into a prince, the prince slaying the dragon. They saw their own lives, their obstacles, their dreams of deliverance. Through four playoff rounds — the conquering of old foes on Long Island, the intensity of five games with the Caps, the supremely dramatic showdown with the Devils, and the final oh-so-difficult step against the Canucks — we grabbed the rope, too. We pulled for them and with them. The opposition always pulled back. Suddenly, we all wore shirts with those diagonal drop-shadow letters. The Stanley Cup became as important to us as it did to the guys playing for it. People couldn't work. For nourishment, we devoured the unprecedented news coverage; for sustenance, we phoned each other in search of reassurance. All we could talk about was the toughness of Kocur, Kypreos, Beukeboom,

Wells, and Lowe; the drive of Nemchinov, Gilbert and Noonan; the heroics of "OT" Matteau; Lidster's revival, Healy's enthusiasm, The Black Aces' dedication, Tikkanen's agitation, Anderson's grit, Kovalev's speed, the persistence of Graves and Zubov, Larmer's amazing versatility, Richter's acrobatics, Leetch's brilliance, and Messier who, after all, was Messier. And when MacTavish hunkered over his stick, stepped into Pavel Bure and drew that last faceoff to the end boards, the buzzer sounded, and the fireworks exploded, we could only say, "I never thought I'd see this."

We never thought we'd see a Rangers captain tour the ice with the Stanley Cup, hand it off to a teammate, who would then hand it off to others. But there it was. There was our dream. We saw the Rangers kiss the Cup and hold it high. We saw it brought to the bench and passed to the coach who held it high, too. We saw it passed to the team president and he, too, hoisted the trophy that for more than a century has been at the center of countless hockey dreams.

We saw it through moist eyes, but we saw it. We saw it. And we cheered in the Garden, we cheered in our homes, we cheered in the streets.

Three days later, the Stanley Cup itself was in the streets and a million and a half people came to cheer the Rangers and cheer themselves. It had started with a parade and it ended with a parade. It was the final "Heave-ho."

At City Hall, there were tributes from the Mayor. Each Ranger got a key to the City. And when it was his turn to get his key, Eddie Olczyk asked to address the crowd. One of the Black Aces who rarely played, Olczyk showed so much dedication this season that his teammates voted him the "Player's Player." And he let us in on a secret, the new chant for 1994-95: "Heave-ho! Two in a row!"

Just once, eh?

Rangers President and General Manager Neil Smith made the moves to bring the Stanley Cup to New York.

OVER THEIR 68 SEASONS, the Rangers have had some historic hockey figures at the helm. Lester Patrick, Frank Boucher, Muzz Patrick, Emile Francis, John Ferguson, Fred Shero, Craig Patrick, and Phil Esposito are all men whose names are linked in various ways to hockey immortality. Yet in the roller coaster world of Ranger fortunes, none has had the immediate success running the club as has **Neil Smith**.

In his five years as general manager, the Rangers have finished first in their division three times and second on another occasion. In two of the last three seasons, they have won the Presidents' Trophy for finishing first overall in the League. In 1994, they reached the Stanley Cup Finals for the first time since 1979. And, of course, they won the top prize for the first time in 54 years.

The club's success reflects Neil's extraordinary ability to recognize talent and his bold, sure hand in making moves necessary to keep the Rangers on course. Through trades, drafts, and free agent signings, he has always worked hard to upgrade the club's level of talent. The results of his efforts carried the Rangers to new heights in the 1993-94 season.

The groundwork for victory began just after the 1992-93 season concluded, when Smith hired Mike Keenan, one of the most successful coaches in NHL history, to pilot the Rangers. It was just the first of Smith's moves that returned the Rangers to the top of the NHL.

By forging a complicated three-way deal with Chicago and Hartford, Smith secured the services of winger Steve Larmer, who for 11 seasons as a Blackhawk had set standards for durability and consistency. Larmer continued his excellent play when he arrived on Broadway.

At the trading deadline, Smith addressed the need to further upgrade the Rangers for the playoffs by pulling off a stunning series of trades. By acquiring Glenn Anderson, Brian Noonan, Craig MacTavish, and Stephane Matteau, Smith added needed size and playoff experience for the final sprint to the Presidents' Trophy and the club's memorable Stanley Cup run.

A championship hockey club needs top-notch leadership on the ice, behind the bench, and in the front office. The Rangers have that leadership in president and general manager Neil Smith.

13

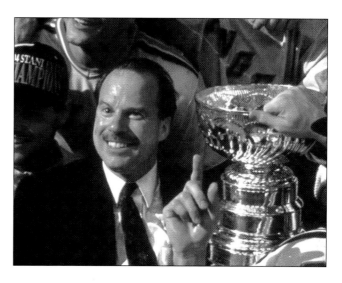

HE'S CEREBRAL, COMPLEX, **COMPETITIVE,** and committed. Most of all, he is a proven winner. When the Rangers hired **Mike Keenan** in April of 1993, they hired a man to guide the team who had won in junior hockey, collegiate hockey, the AHL and the premiere world-class tournament, the Canada Cup. But it was Keenan's NHL resume that was most impressive – a resume he enriched this season.

The Rangers April 8th win against Toronto gave Keenan his third NHL regular-season championship and his sixth division title in nine NHL campaigns. Defeating the Islanders and the Capitals put his team in the Conference Final for the sixth time and beating the Devils signaled his fourth appearance in the Stanley Cup Final. The Rangers' 52-24-8 season gave him a lifetime .599 winning percentage, the fifth highest mark on the all-time list. And by coaching the Rangers to a 3-2 win over Florida on April 4, he moved into tenth place on the all-time career victory list.

But Mike Keenan is the first to say that personal achievements are secondary to team accomplishments. And to that end, he devoted his full attention and enormous energy, spending long hours with the players on the ice and in meetings, designing fitness and motivational programs. With assistant coaches Colin Campbell and Dick Todd, he analyzed opponents and devised tactics that led to a franchise record 52 wins and 112 points in the regular-season and a Stanley Cup playoff run that Rangers fans will never forget.

Assistant coaches Colin Campbell, left; and Dick Todd, center, with Mike Keenan

YOU CAN SEE IT ETCHED ON HIS FACE, the steely, single-minded determination to accomplish a difficult task. You can see it in his movements, forceful and with purpose and certainty. And you can see it in the way others respect and respond to him.

For a dozen seasons **Mark Messier** has been one of hockey's premier power forwards, with trophies, honors, and awards galore. He has scored the big goals, made the big plays, inspired teammates, and won championships. He has taken control of games and shown the way to victory time and again. Not many hockey players can make that claim.

In a season where he quietly fought nagging injury, Messier remained undaunted. He averaged better than a point a game, finishing second in team scoring. He broke into the top ten on the NHL's all-time lists for assists and total points. His historic third-period hat-trick against the New Jersey Devils in Game Six of the Eastern Conference Championship exemplifies Messier's will to lift the Rangers to the Stanley Cup.

There is no finer leader in hockey than Mark Messier.

THE RANGERS RECORD BREAKER

TWENTY-TWO SEASONS AGO, Vic Hadfield became the first Ranger to score 50 goals in a season. No Ranger equalled or passed this total – until this year. On March 23 in Edmonton, **Adam Graves** scored his 50th goal. Three minutes later, he scored his 51st.

Graves finished with 52 goals, tops on the Rangers and fifth-highest in the league. His 20 power play goals also led the club. He made his chances count, scoring goals on better than 17 percent of his shots, the best mark on the club. The Rangers were 33-5-2 in games where Graves scored a goal this season, a statistic which helps explain why he was selected the Rangers' most valuable player.

But it's more than his goal scoring that made Adam Graves the Rangers' MVP, for he is the consummate team player, excelling in every facet of the game. He is quick, he is strong, and he is tough. On the ice, he is a buzzsaw in overdrive, cutting down the opposition, grabbing the puck, taking the hits and making the sacrifices to create the play. These qualities earned Graves the Steven McDonald "Extra Effort" Award for the third consecutive season.

As good as he is on the ice, Adam Graves is equally accomplished off it. Committed to community service and charity work, he is celebrity chairman for Family Dynamics and the Greater New York City Ice Hockey League. In recognition of his concern for others, the NHL named Adam the 1994 recipient of the King Clancy Award for humanitarian service two days after the Rangers won the Stanley Cup. As selfless with his spare time and energy as he is in his career, Adam Graves is a rare individual.

A TEAM'S FORTUNE RISES AND FALLS with the play of its goaltenders. And it's the Rangers' good fortune to have a pair of netminders whose play lifted the club all season.

For **Mike Richter**, his season paralleled the club's success and accomplishments. He set new personal standards for wins (42, tops in the NHL and a new club record), consecutive wins (eight), goals-against average (2.57, fifth best in the NHL) and shutouts (five, tied for the NHL's second-highest total in 1993-94). His 20-game unbeaten streak set a new club record, surpassing Davey Kerr's 19-game streak set in the 1939-40 season. His MVP performance in the All-Star Game at Madison Square Garden was an thrill both for him and for the hometown fans. And his four shutouts in the 1994 playoffs tied the NHL record.

The role of back-up goaltender is never an easy one for a competitive athlete like **Glenn Healy**, but his value to the club was demonstrated time and again in 1993-94. Often playing on the road, where the host club is more aggressive, Healy posted a career-best 3.03 goals-against average. His two shutouts, both on the road, matched his personal single-season high. What statistics don't show is how his relief appearances often helped inject new jump into the team at important moments of games.

Most significantly, Richter and Healy developed a strong relationship in which they supported each other and were the other's biggest cheerleader. They did not cheer alone.

Mike Richter, facing page, and Glenn Healy, below, combined to allow just 2.72 goals-against per game in 1993-94.

THE RANGERS POINTMEN

BEST IN THE **LEAGUE.** That was the Ranger's power play this season, and that was the work of the men on the points.

While other clubs would be happy to have one player with the skills of **Brian Leetch** or **Sergei Zubov**, the Rangers had both of them. Leetch and Zubov formed the league's most feared man-advantage tandem due to superior skating, puckhandling, passing, and shooting skills. Each showed great anticipation in keeping the play alive at the blue line. The results were obvious: Zubov and Leetch both finished among the top five in power play assists, power play points and total points by defensemen.

For Leetch, the season was a return to his 1992 Norris Trophy form. In fact, his all-around defensive play improved this season, as he raised the physical dimension of his game. His offensive numbers remained high with 23 goals (second among NHL defensemen) and 79 points (fourth among league defensemen). He was on the ice for 87 of the Rangers' 96 power play goals and, at even strength, his plus-28 was the best plus/minus rating on the club.

Zubov was a revelation this season. With 12 goals and 89 points, he was the league's second highest-scoring defenseman and became the first defenseman in NHL history to finish as the scoring leader for the team that finished first overall in the standings. His 77 assists were best on the club and fourth highest in the League. He is one of only five defensemen in team history to register 50-or-more assists in a single season and, along with Leetch, is one of only two to record at least 70 assists.

It wasn't wise to take too many penalties against the Rangers this season. The play of Leetch and Zubov made that point loud and clear.

Sergei Zubov, above, was the Rangers top scorer in 1993-94. Brian Leetch, below, won the Conn Smythe Trophy as the MVP of the 1994 playoffs.

THE GUYS WHO TAKE CARE OF BUSINESS in their own end may not get the headlines, but as any hockey coach will tell you, championships are won with strong defense. The 1993-94 Rangers built and maintained a strong defense corps. The club allowed the third fewest goals-against during the 84-game regular season and limited its opposition to no more than three goals on 59 occasions. The Rangers roster included a number of veteran blueliners who played a stay-at-home style with intelligence and poise.

For more than a dozen years, **Kevin Lowe** has been one of the NHL's top one-on-one defensemen, with the ability to bring his performance up a notch in the big games. An excellent penalty killer and shot blocker, his leadership also provided a stabilizing force that aided Sergei Zubov's development.

Jeff Beukeboom, one of the hardest checkers in the game, often lifted his teammates and the Garden crowd with big hits at key moments. He keeps the front of the net clear and plays his angles well, making it hard for the opposition to go around him.

The kind of tough, physical player who would have flourished in the old six-team NHL, **Jay Wells** can be counted on for a few big hits every game. He gets lots of respect in front of the net and is adept at moving the puck up ice. His 15 years of NHL experience are a great asset in the dressing room.

Doug Lidster displays good skills in every aspect of the game. He's steady and dependable in his own end, can play the point on the power play and kill penalties. He stepped into the lineup for the club's comeback against the Devils and also scored the crucial first goal in Game Two of the Stanley Cup finals.

Having played over 100 games at the international level, **Alexander Karpovtsev** puts those lessons to work for the Rangers, showing a knack for reading the play and reacting to it.

In **Mattias Norstrom**, far left, and **Joby Messier**, left, the Rangers have two eager youngsters with size and strength who have given the team depth on defense. Both could earn regular blueline spots in the seasons ahead.

THE
ARTISTS

THEY ARE THE **B**IG **P**LAY GUYS. They set up plays and they finish them. Their skills with the puck can lift fans out of their seats. Every team has its artists, but the Rangers are lucky enough to have many of them. On top of that, the Rangers' artists are far more than one-dimensional players.

Esa Tikkanen gives Mike Keenan great flexibility because he can play any forward position and performs at a high level in both offensive and defensive situations. His shot is one of the best on the team and he is feisty, getting under the skin of opposing players.

Twenty-one year old **Alexei Kovalev** blossomed this season into one of the game's most electrifying performers. With sure hands, swift feet, and a quick shot, he can alter a game's momentum. He loves to play hockey.

He played for years without receiving the recognition he deserved, but **Steve Larmer** is as complete a player as there is in the NHL. A top-notch shooter and special team player, he uses the rink like a chess board.

Sergei Nemchinov goes about his job more quietly than most, but is no less a consummate hockey player. He possesses deceptive speed, good hands, an excellent shot, and good defensive instincts.

An injury kept gifted scorer Eddie Olczyk out of the lineup for much of the season but, working hard to stay in shape, he earned great respect from his teammates who voted him winner of the Players' Player Award.

THE RANGERS
THE ENERGIZERS

FREQUENTLY DURING THE COURSE of the long season, a hockey club needs a jump start, a shot of adrenaline to get its game back in high gear. Sometimes a goal will do it, sometimes a save. And sometimes a good hardworking shift, where players bang bodies or inject some needed speed, will turn the momentum of a game. The players who can grind out a super-shift on demand do so by pressuring their opponents and creating turnovers, thereby giving their teammates a lift. They may not make the scoring summary as often as the artists, but the role they play is no less essential in achieving victory.

Greg Gilbert has more than 700 games of NHL experience in which he has parlayed solid physical play and a deceptively hard shot into dependable performances.

With a well-earned reputation as one of hockey's tough guys, **Joe Kocur** has also worked hard to become a more effective hockey player, clearing the zone, forechecking with tenacity and developing a hard shot.

Aggressive **Nick Kypreos** is a good checker who is also adept with the puck around the net, willing to withstand a pounding to gain position and make the play in front.

Speedy **Mike Hudson**, left, is a versatile forward who can play either center or left wing. Hard working **Mike Hartman**, right, is a heart-and-soul type of player. Both spent long stretches out of the lineup in 1993-94, but their dedication to off-ice conditioning and preparation impressed the coaching staff and gave the club needed depth during the season.

THE **STANLEY CUP PLAYOFFS** are the most grueling championship in professionals sports. Players and teams are subjected to two months of the most intense mental and physical pressure they will ever face. To advance to the Stanley Cup Final in today's NHL, teams must have more size, strength, and toughness than in previous years. For players and coaches, having performed at that level in the past is a great aid in coping with the pressures. When Neil Smith acquired four players at the trading deadline, he not only made deals for physical players with good skills, he also got a quartet with plenty of experience in important games

● ● ●

Everyone expects offense from **Glenn Anderson**, but he is also a battler and a confident player who brings an element of versatility to the game. He has good playmaking instincts and, with his strong skating ability and penchant for physical play, he goes hard to the net and makes things happen.

Stephane Matteau has great size and strength, which he puts to good use in the corners and in front of the net. Combined with his ability to tip in shots and handle the puck intelligently in front of the net, he became a welcome addition to the power play. His two overtime goals against the Devils epitomized his value in the playoffs.

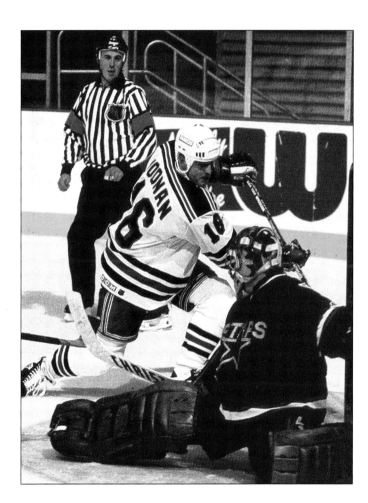

A player who can get hot and be a dominant figure in the team's offensive production, **Brian Noonan**, right, can also make valuable contributions in numerous other situations. He is a deceptively fast skater, and a creative playmaker coming out of the corners with the puck.

Craig MacTavish has digested the lessons of his 900-plus NHL games and puts those lessons to work as an accomplished defensive forward. He plays well in big games, even getting the occasional big goal to go along with his faceoff, penalty killing, and forechecking expertise.

33

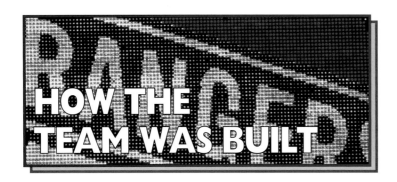

HOW THE TEAM WAS BUILT

June 15, 1985 • Drafted goaltender **Mike Richter** 28th overall in the second round of the NHL Entry Draft.

June 21, 1986 • Drafted defenseman **Brian Leetch** ninth overall in the first round of the NHL Entry Draft.

June 17, 1989 • Drafted defenseman **Joby Messier** 118th overall in the sixth round of the NHL Entry Draft.

July 17, 1989 • Hired general manager **Neil Smith**.

June 16, 1990 • Drafted defenseman **Sergei Zubov** 85th overall in the fifth round of the NHL Entry Draft. Drafted forward **Sergei Nemchinov** in the 12th round 244th pick overall, of the NHL Entry Draft.

March 5, 1991 • Acquired forward **Joe Kocur** from the Detroit Red Wings along with Per Djoos in exchange for Kevin Miller, Dennis Vial and Jim Cummins.

Brian Leetch, drafted 9th overall in 1986.

June 9, 1991 • Drafted forward **Alexei Kovalev** 15th overall in the first round of the NHL Entry Draft. Drafted **Corey Hirsch** 169th overall in the eighth round of the NHL Entry Draft.

September 3, 1991 • Signed forward **Adam Graves** as a free agent. Troy Mallette was sent to the Edmonton Oilers as compensation.

October 4, 1991 • Acquired forward **Mark Messier** from the Edmonton Oilers along with future considerations in exchange for Bernie Nicholls, Steven Rice and Louie DeBrusk.

November 12, 1991 • Acquired defenseman **Jeff Beukeboom** from the Edmonton Oilers for David Shaw and for the future considerations owed to the Oilers as part of the Messier trade of October 4, 1991.

March 9, 1992 • Acquired defenseman **Jay Wells** from the Buffalo Sabres in exchange for Randy Moller.

June 20, 1992 • Drafted defenseman **Mattias Norstrom** 48th overall in the second round of the NHL Entry Draft.

December 11, 1992 • Acquired defenseman **Kevin Lowe** from the Edmonton Oilers in exchange for Roman Oksyuta and the Rangers' third-round draft choice (Alexander Kerch) in the 1993 NHL Entry Draft.

December 28, 1992 • Acquired forward **Ed Olczyk** from the Winnipeg Jets in exchange for Tie Domi and Kris King.

March 17, 1993 • Acquired forward **Esa Tikkanen** from the Edmonton Oilers in exchange for Doug Weight.

March 22, 1993 • Acquired forward **Mike Hartman** from the Tampa Bay Lightning in exchange for Randy Gilhen.

April 17, 1993 • Hired coach **Mike Keenan**.

Mark Messier, acquired from Edmonton on October 4, 1991.

June 25, 1993 • Acquired defenseman **Doug Lidster** from the Vancouver Canucks in exchange for John Vanbiesbrouck. Acquired goaltender **Glenn Healy** from the Tampa Bay Lightning in exhange for the return of Tampa Bay's third round choice in the 1993 Entry Draft. Tampa Bay's draft choice had been obtained by the Rangers as compensation for the Lightning signing Rob Zamuner as a free agent on July 13, 1992.

July 29, 1993 • Signed forward **Greg Gilbert** as a free agent.

September 9, 1993 • Acquired defenseman **Alexander Karpovtsev** from the Quebec Nordiques in exhange for Mike Hurlbut

Neil Smith announced Mike Keenan's signing after the 1992-93 season.

October 3, 1993 • Claimed forward **Mike Hudson** from the Edmonton Oilers in the NHL Waiver Draft.

November 2, 1993 • Acquired forwards **Steve Larmer** and **Nick Kypreos** along with **Barry Richter** and a pick in the 1994 NHL Entry Draft from the Hartford Whalers in exchange for James Patrick and Darren Turcotte.

March 21, 1994 • Acquired forwards **Stephane Matteau** and **Brian Noonan** from the Chicago Blackhawks in exchange for Tony Amonte and the rights to Matt Oates. Acquired forward **Glenn Anderson** along with the rights to Scott Malone and a fourth-round choice in the 1994 NHL Entry Draft from the Toronto Maple Leafs in exchange for Mike Gartner. Acquired forward **Craig MacTavish** from the Edmonton Oilers in exchange for Todd Marchant.

THE 1993-94
SEASON

A REMARKABLE SEASON began in a unique fashion for the New York Rangers when the team traveled to London, England. Twenty-six players, plus coaches, management, and families spent six days in London, practicing three times and then participating in a two-game weekend exhibition tournament against the Toronto Maple Leafs on September 11 and 12 at Wembley Arena.

They also made promotional appearances, were guest stars at youth hockey clinics, and toured some of London's historic sights, including Buckingham Palace, Westminster Abbey, Piccadilly Circus, and Parliament.

At the Lee Valley Ice Arena, the club got a first taste of Mike Keenan's high-intensity, quick-tempo practice style, designed to emphasize conditioning for the long season ahead. They were also introduced to a new set of expectations from the coach, emphasizing commitment, concentration, cooperation and communication with one target in mind – winning the Stanley Cup.

For the players, the three Lee Valley sessions brought the club back together in unique circumstances. Not only were the Rangers opening their training camp in Europe, but these first sessions were held with a much smaller group of players than usually participates in a standard NHL camp. This allowed the club's nucleus to begin healing the psychological wounds that followed their disappointing 1992-93 season in which the club finished last in its division. The London experience allowed the Rangers to take important first steps toward a successful 1993-94 campaign.

Even though the Wembley games were

London's largest rink, the 9,000 seat Wembley Arena, below, hosted the Rangers and Maple Leafs in two September exhibition games.

exhibition contests, the Rangers and Leafs played spectacular hockey with great intensity and dedication. The Rangers swept the series, and the winner-take-all prize of $50,000, by defeating the Leafs 5-3 on Saturday and 3-1 on Sunday.

After accepting the French's Challenge Trophy on behalf of the Rangers, captain Mark Messier remarked that the team wanted to win the exhibition tournament because "It's the first thing we can win."

He said they also wanted to win the NHL's regular-season title and the Stanley Cup. "I think you've got to talk about it. You can't be afraid of it. You've got to envision it. You've got to think about it. You've got to live it. You've got to dream about it. And you've got to make it happen. It's been made very clear to us what the goal is this year. We're going to take it one day at a time and try to build to get there."

The man who set the goal, Mike Keenan, said, "To win the Stanley Cup is a formidable task, but we feel we're up to it. We have a long way to go, we have plenty to learn, an extreme amount of development to take place in the organization. But one of the reasons I was excited about coming to the Rangers was that there was a challenge that hadn't been met in a number of years."

London was an important beginning.

Above: Sergei Nemchinov signs autographs for young British players at a hockey clinic. The Rangers had last played in England as part of a European exhibition tour in 1959.

Below: Kevin Lowe upends Leaf captain Wendel Clark in the first of two exhibition games the teams played in London.

October 5 • The Rangers open their 68th season with a 4-3 loss to Boston.

October 7 • Greg Gilbert skates in his 700th NHL game, a 5-4 win over Tampa Bay.

October 11 • Above: Brian Leetch equals his career high with four assists in a 5-2 win over Washington.

October 13 • Above: The Rangers score a team record six straight power play goals including the game-winner by Alexander Karpovtsev in a 6-4 win over Quebec. Karpovtsev's goal is his first NHL marker.

October 15 • Adam Graves' early shorthanded goal sparks a 5-2 win in Buffalo.

October 24 • Above: Esa Tikkanen's third-period goal defeats the Kings 3-2 and ends the Rangers' three-game losing streak.

October 28 • Lower left: Two late goals, including one by Adam Graves with ten seconds remaining, give the Rangers a 3-3 tie with the defending Cup champions, the Montreal Canadiens

October 30 • Adam Graves scores twice and Sergei Zubov adds three assists in a 4-1 win in Hartford.

October 31 • Sergei Nemchinov scores twice as the Rangers defeat the Devils 4-1 in a neutral site game played in Halifax, Nova Scotia.

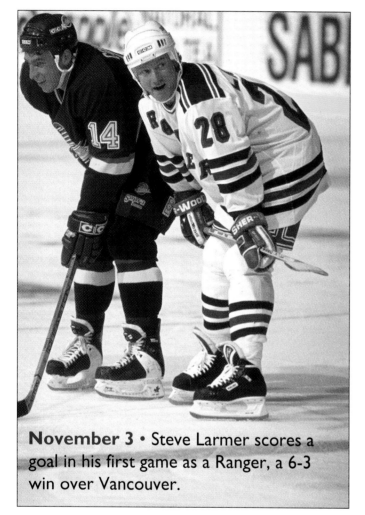

November 3 • Steve Larmer scores a goal in his first game as a Ranger, a 6-3 win over Vancouver.

November 6 • Steve Larmer gets three assists in a 4-2 win in Quebec.

November 8 • Steve Larmer scores twice in a 6-3 win over Tampa Bay.

November 10 • Adam Graves has a goal and an assist in a 2-1 win over Winnipeg.

November 13 • In the Rangers' seventh straight win, Mike Richter stops 27 shots shutting out Washington 2-0. The Rangers survive their 23rd consecutive shorthanded situation without allowing a goal.

November 14 • Jeff Beukeboom, above, records his first career two-goal game and his 100th career point in the Rangers' 3-3 tie with San Jose. This marks the club's tenth consecutive game without a loss.

November 16 • Brian Leetch records a goal and an assist in a 4-2 win over the Panthers in Florida.

November 19 • Jay Wells plays his 900th NHL game. Adam Graves and Esa Tikkanen, above, score twice as the Rangers get four straight goals in 5-3 win over Tampa Bay. The victory moves the Rangers into first place in the Eastern Conference. The club would stay in first for the balance of the season.

November 23 • Right: Ed Olczyk scores the game winner and Larmer skates in his 900th NHL game, a 5-4 victory over Montreal.

November 24 • Left: Sergei Zubov opened the scoring with a power play goal in a 7-1 win in Ottawa. The victory extended the Rangers' undefeated streak to 14 games. This would prove to be the NHL's longest undefeated streak in 1993-94.

November 28 • Mark Messier scores a goal and adds two assists in a 3-1 win over Washington.

November 30 • Brian Leetch scores two goals in a 3-1 win at New Jersey.

November • With a 9-0-1 record, a 2.37 goals against average and a .917 save percentage, Mike Richter, left, was named NHL Player of the Month for November.

December 4 • Mark Messier collects assists on the tying and winning goals, including the 800th assist of his career, in a 4-3 win at Toronto.

December 5 • The Rangers defeat New Jersey 2-1, running their home undefeated streak to 10 games.

December 13 • Mike Richter stops 28 shots in a 2-0 shutout of Buffalo. The team's record of 21-6-3 for 45 points ties the franchise mark for most points after 30 games first set in 1971-72.

December 15 • The Rangers beat Hartford 5-2 and Mike Richter ties Davey Kerr's 1939-40 team record with a 19-game unbeaten streak.

December 19 • Above: Defeating Ottawa 6-3, Mike Richter sets a new club record with a 20-game undefeated streak.

December 23 • Right: Glenn Healy makes 20 saves as he shuts out Washington. Adam Graves scores the only goal of the game in the third period.

December 26 • Mike Gartner, above, scores the 600th goal of his NHL career. The Rangers extend their home unbeaten streak to 15 games by scoring a season-high eight goals in an 8-3 win over New Jersey.

December 29 • With an injured wrist sidelining Mark Messier, Esa Tikkanen leads the way, collecting two goals and an assist in a 4-3 win in St. Louis.

January 3 • The Rangers fire a season high 54 shots on goal, defeating Florida 3-2 on Adam Graves' third-period tally. The win is the club's 16th consecutive home game without a loss.

January 14 • Brian Leetch and Adam Graves each record a goal and assist in a 5-2 win over Philadelphia.

January 16 • Above: Returning from an injury ahead of schedule, Steve Larmer rejoins the club and scores a penalty shot goal as he and Mike Keenan celebrated their return to Chicago with a 5-1 win.

January 18 • Just before the All-Star break, Sergei Nemchinov, above, registers a goal and an assist in a 4-1 win over St. Louis.

January 25 • Top right: The Rangers match their highest output for the season in an 8-3 win at San Jose. Steve Larmer has two goals and an assist, Sergei Zubov's four assists set career highs for points and assists in a game, and Kevin Lowe notches a pair of assists, including his 400th career point.

January 27 • Right: With two seconds remaining in overtime, Mark Messier's dramatic goal gives the Rangers a 5-4 win over the Kings in Los Angeles.

January 31 • Right: With a goal and an assist in a 5-3 win against Pittsburgh, Mark Messier moves past Alex Delvecchio into sole possession of tenth place on the NHL's all-time scoring list.

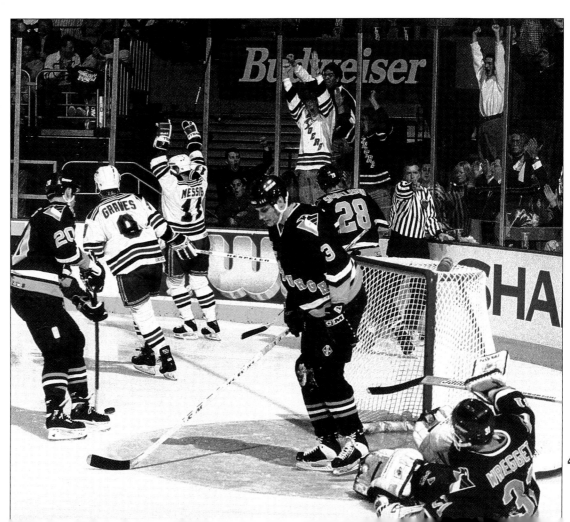

47

THE NEW YORK RANGERS and Madison Square Garden hosted the NHL's 45th All-Star Game on January 22, and the event turned into a celebration, not only of hockey's finest, but also of the home team's top players. The Rangers contributed four players – more than any other team in the League – to the Eastern Conference squad as Mark Messier, Brian Leetch, Adam Graves, and Mike Richter played like All-Stars in the East's 9-8 victory.

For Messier, it was his 12th appearance in an NHL All-Star Game. He served as captain for the Eastern Conference and was selected to start the game when Jaromir Jagr was sidelined with an injury. Messier scored a goal against San Jose's Arturs Irbe in the second period and also added an assist.

Leetch was voted to the starting team for the Eastern Conference by fans around the League and made his fourth All-Star appearance. He was on the ice for three Eastern Conference goals, including the tying marker in the East's final spurt to victory.

Graves, making his first All-Star appearance, got two assists and led all players in the game with eight shots on goal. Playing on a line with Messier and New York-born Joe Mullen, Graves combined with Messier to set up Mullen for an early third-period goal that kept the East within striking distance in this see-saw encounter.

But the biggest star of the game was Mike Richter, whose acrobatics stopped 19 of 21 shots during the second period. He stymied Pavel Bure on five high-quality scoring opportunities, including four breakaways, and stopped Teemu Selanne on three big chances. Richter's heroics sparked chants of "Let's Go Rangers!" and "Rich-ter! Rich-ter!" from the home town crowd.

Richter's performance earned All-Star MVP honors. He was the third Ranger to win the award and he drove off with a new truck as the winner's prize. Leetch summed it up for everyone when he said, "It was fun. The Ranger fans are awfully loyal. They gave us a lot of support and I think we gave them a good show."

Mike Richter, right, faced a 21-shot barrage in the second period that included more than a dozen superb scoring chances. Selected as the MVP of the game, he was presented with a truck in an on-ice ceremony.

Below: The Rangers' four Eastern Conference All-Stars: from left, Adam Graves, Mark Messier, Richter and Brian Leetch.

Opposite page: Mark Messier upped his career All-Star scoring total to 10 points with a goal and an assist in the 1994 game.

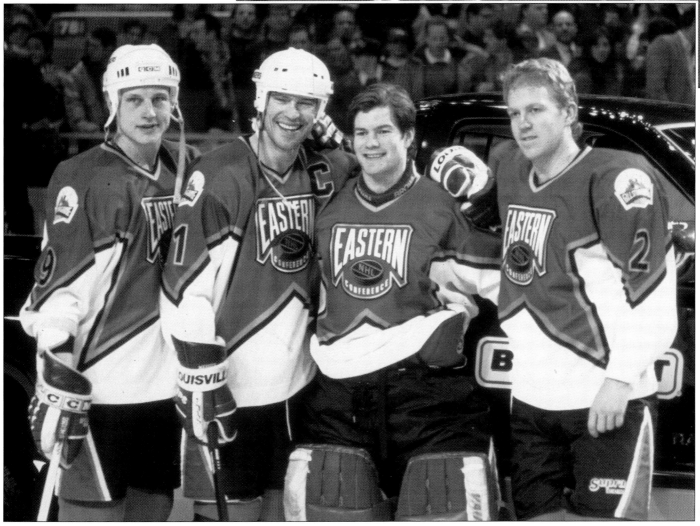

February 7 • In a 4-1 loss to the Washington Capitals, the Rangers set a club record for most shorthanded goals in a season with 15.

February 11 • Right: The hard winter of 1994 took its toll on the city as snow caused the first postponement of a Rangers game in the history of Madison Square Garden.

February 14 • The Rangers kill 11 of the Nordiques' 12 power plays and get a shorthanded goal by Mark Messier to win in Quebec 4-2.

February 2 • In a 4-4 tie with the Islanders, Adam Graves scores three goals and Mark Messier adds four assists to move into 11th place on the NHL's all-time assist list with 815.

February 3 • Right: Because his regular facemask had broken, Glenn Healy covers the helmet of his white practice mask with blue tape and wears it to shut out the Bruins 3-0. The game marks the Rangers' first shutout in Boston since 1967. The win brings the Rangers' record to 7-1-1 over their previous nine games.

February 28 • Playing their seventh game in 11 days, the Rangers defeat Philadelphia 4-1 as Mike Richter records his 100th career victory.

February 18 • Mike Richter shuts out Ottawa 3-0 as Adam Graves scores twice.

February 21 • A 4-3 win against Pittsburgh gives the Rangers their fourth win in the last five games.

February 23 • In a 6-3 loss to Boston, Brian Leetch gets two assists, giving him 424 career points and moving him past Dean Prentice into 11th place on the Rangers all-time scoring list.

February 24 • Right: With four minutes remaining in the third period, Greg Gilbert's brilliant backhanded redirection of a shot by Kevin Lowe clinches a 3-1 victory over the Devils. Sergei Zubov also had a goal and two assists in this game.

March 2 • Mark Messier's two assists in a 5-2 win over Quebec move him past Alex Delvecchio into tenth place on the NHL's all-time assist list.

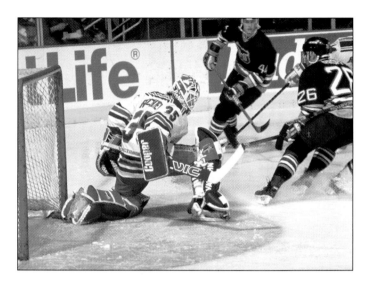

March 16 • Above: Mike Richter's fourth shutout of the season leads the Rangers past Hartford 4-0. The win is the club's 44th of the season

March 5 • With just over a minute left, Sergei Zubov's power play goal gives the Rangers a 5-4 win over the Islanders, their first win on Long Island since 1989.

March 9 • Mike Gartner's 611th goal moves him past Bobby Hull into fifth place on the NHL's all-time goal-scoring list. Sergei Nemchinov has two goals and an assist in a 7-5 neutral site win over Washington in Halifax.

March 22 • Above: Playing in his first game as a Ranger, Stephane Matteau (32) scores with 14 seconds remaining in regulation time to tie the Flames 4-4 in Calgary.

March 23 • Adam Graves breaks the Rangers' single-season goal-scoring record. Both his 50th goal, top, and his 51st, bottom, came in a 5-3 win at Edmonton.

March 25 • In a 5-2 victory over Vancouver, Brian Leetch scores two goals, including the 100th of his career, to join James Patrick and Ron Greschner as the third defenseman in Ranger history to reach this plateau.

March 29 • Below: The Rangers bench celebrates Alexei Kovalev's last-minute goal in a 4-3 win over the Flyers in Philadelphia. The win gives the Rangers 100 points on the season and sets a franchise record with their 23rd road victory of the season.

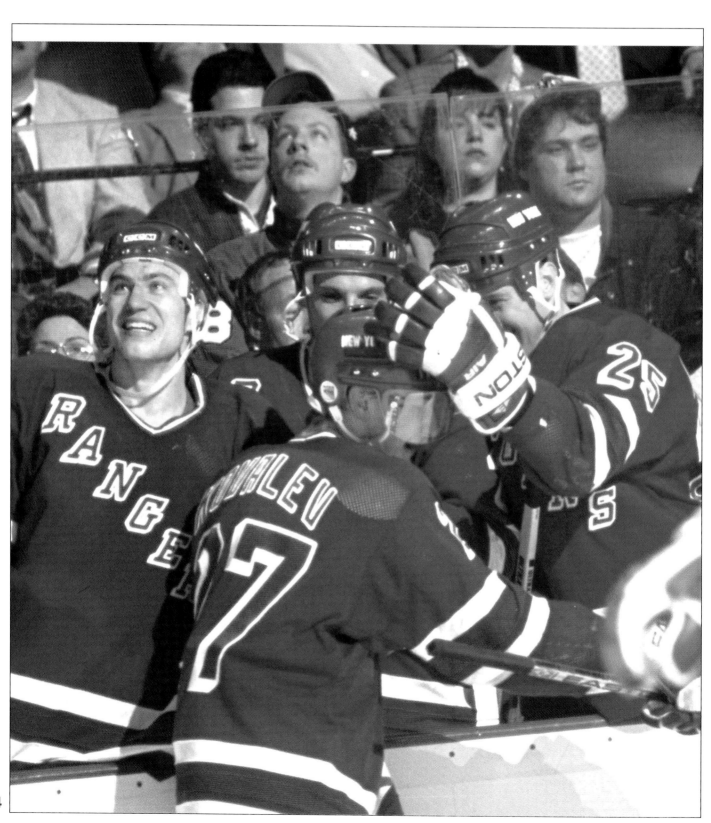

April 1 • Mike Richter's fifth shutout of the season, 3-0 over Dallas, gives him 38 wins on the season, breaking Ed Giacomin's 1968-69 mark of 37 to establish a franchise record.

April 2 • Right: Craig MacTavish's goal caps a four-goal rally to overcome the Devils 4-2 in New Jersey.

April 3 • Mike Richter is named NHL Player of the Week.

April 4 • Mike Keenan moves past Emile Francis into tenth place on the NHL's all-time win list for coaches, recording his 394th win in the 3-2 victory over Florida.

April 8 • After defeating Toronto 5-3, the Rangers clinch the Presidents' Trophy, setting a new team record with their 51st win of the season. Right: NHL senior vice president Brian Burke presents the trophy to Mark Messier.

RANGERS

APRIL

April 10 • Sergei Zubov tallies three assists in a 5-4 loss to the Islanders, moving him past Brian Leetch (1990-91) and Mark Messier (1991-92) for the second-highest single-season assist total in club history. He would finish the season with 77 assists.

April 12 • The Rangers score three third-period goals to defeat Buffalo 3-2 and set an all-time franchise record for points in a season with 111, surpassing the previous mark of 109 set in 1970-71 and equaled in 1971-72. Brian Noonan, below, scores the game-winning goal.

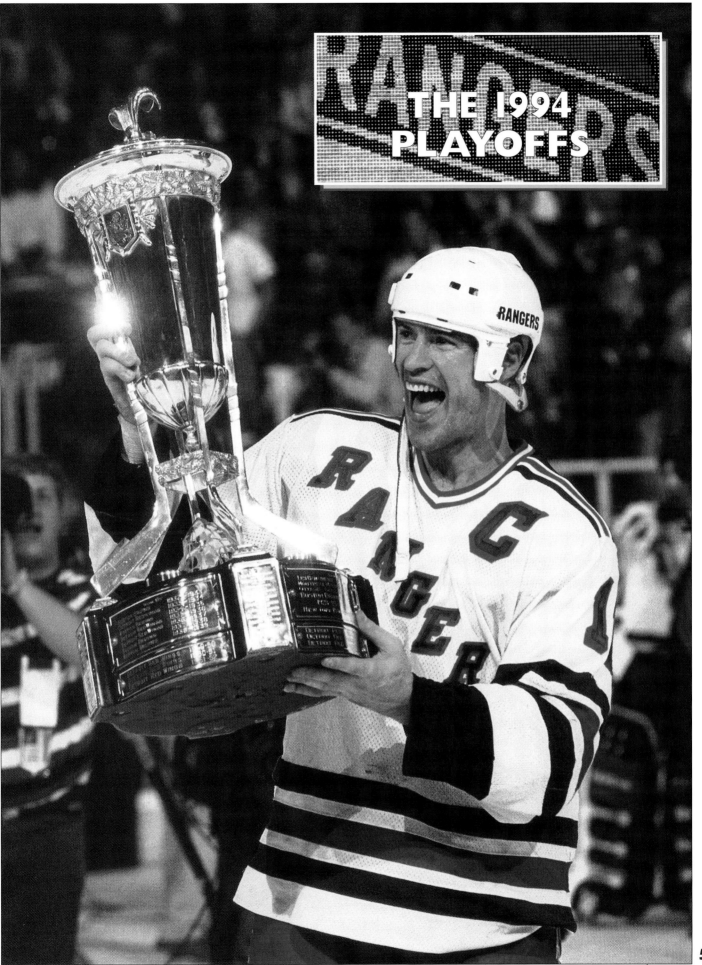

THE 1994 PLAYOFFS

A MID HEADLINES READING "SWEEPING STATEMENT," "4-GETABOUTIT" and "Four-gone Conclusion," Rangers fans rejoiced at the outcome of the eighth Rangers–Islanders playoff matchup. In a convincing, well-rounded display that made the hockey world take notice, the Rangers downed the Islanders in four games, outscoring their arch-rivals 22-3. The 19-goal differential was the second-highest four-game margin in Stanley Cup history, one goal short of the Boston Bruins' 20 goal margin (28-8) against the St. Louis Blues in 1972. It was the second four-game sweep in franchise history, the first being in 1972 against Chicago.

It was a complete team effort in which 11 different players scored goals and the Rangers limited the Islanders to 90 shots over the four games. Mike Richter stopped 87 of them and posted twin 6-0 shutouts in the opening two games, the first time in 11 years and only the ninth time in NHL history that a club started the playoffs with consecutive shutouts. The Rangers previously turned the trick in 1929 when John Ross Roach shut out the New York Americans. The only other time in club history a goalie earned back-to-back playoff shutouts occurred in 1940, when Davey Kerr blanked the Bruins twice by identical 1-0 scores in the semi-finals.

The Rangers special teams were truly special in the sweep. They scored eight goals in 27 power play opportunities and killed 16 of the 17 Islander advantages.

Brian Leetch opened the scoring in round one of the playoffs.

GAME ONE
April 17, at Madison Square Garden
Rangers 6 • Islanders 0

P RIOR TO THE GAME, BRIAN LEETCH LATER ADMITTED that many of the Rangers had been nervous. "But guys like MacT, Kevin Lowe and Mess, they didn't seem like it was any different than the regular season," he said. "They were like, 'Let's play. This is what we've been working for all season, so let's have fun.'" Leetch's own nervousness had vanished by the time his power play wrist shot through a screen opened the scoring at 3:32. It was the first of many early-game playoff goals the Rangers would score. Before the first period, ended Steve Larmer added a power play goal of his own, skating out from behind the net and snapping off a quick 15-footer to the long side past Ron Hextall at 15:28.

Those goals were a prelude to the Rangers' explosive second period, which put the game away. The

Game One • April 17, 1994
Rangers 6, Islanders 0
FIRST PERIOD
1) NYR Leetch 1 (Messier, Zubov) (PPG) 3:32
2) NYR Larmer 1 (Zubov, Kovalev) (PPG) 15:28
PENALTIES – Lowe NYR (holding the stick) 1:16; Krupp NYI (hooking) 3:14; Gilbert NYR (interference) 7:31; Malakhov NYI (holding) 14:18; Ferraro NYI (slashing) 17:26.

SECOND PERIOD
3) NYR Messier 1 (Graves) 9:13
4) NYR Graves 1 (Messier, Beukeboom) 12:19
5) NYR Kovalev 1 (Larmer) 14:05
6) NYR Zubov 1 (Matteau, Leetch) 17:38
PENALTIES – Beukeboom NYR (interference) 7:37; Thomas NYI (hooking) 7:51; Ferraro NYI (roughing), Noonan NYR (roughing) 11:35; Kurvers NYI (highsticking) 15:38.

THIRD PERIOD
No scoring.
PENALTIES – Graves NYR (roughing) 4:55; Dalgarno NYI (unsportsmanlike conduct), Beukeboom NYR (unsportsmanlike conduct) 6:30; Acton NYI (slashing) 8:35; Matteau NYR (interference on the goaltender) 10:10; Hogue NYI (interference) 11:44; Kaminsky NYI (highsticking - double minor) 15:31.

Shots on goal	1	2	3	T
NY ISLANDERS	8	8	5	21
NY RANGERS	11	19	9	39

Goaltenders	TIME	SV	GA	ENG	W/L
NYI Hextall	(37:38)	22	6	0	L
NYI McLennan	(22:22)	11	0	0	-
NYR Richter	(60:00)	21	0	0	W

PP Conversions NYI 0/5 NYR 2/9

Referee: Don Koharski.
Linesmen: Dan McCourt, Dan Schachte.
Attendance: 18,200.

backbreaker came at 9:13 when Adam Graves dropped a pass to Messier who threw it on the net from near the left wing boards. The shot surprised goalie Ron Hextall and squeaked through his pads. Three minutes later, it became 4-0 when Graves' own rebound hit him in the cheek and went in past Hextall. Two minutes later, Alexei Kovalev split the defense on a perfect pass from Steve Larmer and beat Hextall on the breakaway. Sergei Zubov, who assisted on the two power play goals, closed out the scoring at 17:38 on a long wrist shot from the high slot.

Zubov's goal also closed out Hextall who was replaced for the balance of the game by Jamie McLennan. The line of Craig MacTavish, Brian Noonan and Esa Tikkanen shut down the Islanders top threat Pierre Turgeon and his wingers Steve Thomas and Derek King.

The Rangers allowed the Islanders little room to maneuver in Game Two.

GAME TWO
April 18, at Madison Square Garden
Rangers 6 • Islanders 0

HOPING A CHANGE OF GOALTENDERS would change their luck, the Isles started McLennan and came out strong, outshooting the Rangers 13-1 in the first half of the period. "The story tonight was Mike Richter in the first ten minutes," Mike Keenan said after the game. "We knew they would come at us very hard and I think he was the key in stabilizing our team and giving us a chance to regroup." While Richter's work kept the Isles at bay, the only early Ranger shot resulted in a goal. Brian Leetch, defending against an Islander rush, stopped Yan Kaminsky in his tracks, pushed him out of the zone into center ice, grabbed the puck, skated over the blue line and then fed an unchecked Alexei Kovalev, who whipped a quick shot behind McLennan at 5:41.

The momentum shifted to the Rangers in the latter stages of the first period and they again exploded in the second, ignited by Glenn Anderson. Directly after the opening faceoff, he intercepted a clearing pass by Dennis Vaske and fed Messier who beat McLennan on a breakaway. Eighty seconds later, with Stephane Matteau providing a distraction in front of the net, Kevin Lowe cashed in a Kovalev rebound to make it 3-0. MacTavish made it 4-0 at 12:29 after he stickchecked the puck from Turgeon to Tikkanen who fed Noonan to create a two-on-one break with MacTavish. Noonan's shot was

stopped but MacTavish stabbed the rebound in behind McLennan.

MacTavish started the next scoring play as well, stealing the puck from King and passing cross ice to Alexander Karpovtsev. His shot deflected off Matteau's knee into the net. At 4:23 of the third, Noonan grabbed the rebound of a Graves shot and deposited a backhander into the Islanders' net for the sixth goal.

GAME THREE
April 21, at Nassau Coliseum
Rangers 5 • Islanders 1

WITH HEXTALL BACK IN GOAL, the Rangers wasted little time in re-asserting their dominance, scoring on their first two shots of the game. Noonan head-manned a pass to Tikkanen, who scored on a low slapshot from inside the blueline at 2:08 of the first period. On the power play a minute and a half later, Leetch's screen shot from the left point made it 2-0.

Midway through the second period, the Rangers scored their 15th consecutive goal of the series when Graves took a perfect feed in the slot from Leetch and wristed the puck into the net on a power play. Ray Ferraro gave the Isles their first goal of the series about five minutes later, poking in a rebound during a wild scramble in which both Richter and Sergei Nemchinov were playing without their sticks.

The Isles started to build momentum and Richter made a big save on a shot by Travis Green, but shortly thereafter, Hextall was called for delay of game when his clearing attempt sailed into the crowd. On the resulting power play, Kovalev finished a fine passing play between Zubov, Leetch, and Matteau with a shot from the slot at 18:48. Graves closed out the scoring with an unassisted powerplay goal after he stole the puck, skated around Dave Chyzowski and fired a shot past Hextall from the right faceoff circle. Still sharp, Richter

Game Three • April 21, 1994
Rangers 5, Islanders 1
FIRST PERIOD
1) NYR Tikkanen 1 (Noonan, Leetch) 2:08
2) NYR Leetch 2 (Messier, Noonan) (PPG) 3:40
PENALTIES – Thomas NYI (holding the stick) 3:26; Krupp NYI (cross-checking) 7:07; Wells NYR (hooking) 13:00.
SECOND PERIOD
3) NYR Graves 2 (Leetch, Zubov) (PPG) 10:43
4) NYI Ferraro 1 (Dalgarno, Vaske) 15:28
5) NYR Kovalev 3 (Matteau, Leetch) (PPG) 18:48
PENALTIES – Ferraro NYI (tripping) 9:25; Noonan NYR (roughing), Hogue NYI (roughing) 15:54; Hextall NYI (delay of game - served by McInnis) 17:25.
THIRD PERIOD
6) NYR Graves 3 10:37
PENALTIES – Kovalev NYR (highsticking) 7:09; Noonan NYR (slashing) 11:32; Acton NYI (roughing) 14:50; Green NYI (tripping) 15:41; Thomas NYI (cross-checking) 19:26.

Shots on goal	1	2	3	T
NY RANGERS	3	10	5	18
NY ISLANDERS	4	10	8	22

Goaltenders	TIME	SV	GA	ENG	W/L
NYR Richter	(60:00)	21	1	0	W
NYI Hextall	(60:00)	13	5	0	L

PP CONVERSIONS   NYR 3/7   NYI 0/3
Referee: Dan Marouelli.
Linesmen: Ray Scapinello, Ron Asselstine.
Attendance: 16,297.

Adam Graves, checked here by Steve Thomas, scored two goals in Game Three.

made big stops toward the end of the game and the Rangers penalty killers remained perfect for the series, having killed off 15 consecutive manpower advantages.

After the game, Kevin Lowe told reporters the goal differential "is indicative of the respect we have for them. We're digging in and playing as hard as we can defensively, and sometimes a good offense is a good defense. We're trying to force mistakes and force goals. It's a lot easier to play with a lead."

GAME FOUR
April 24, at Nassau Coliseum
Rangers 5 • Islanders 2

FACING ELIMINATION, THE ISLES CAME OUT STORMING, jumping to a 2-0 lead early in the first period. Thomas scored the Isles' first power play goal of the series on a rebound at 1:28. Six minutes later, Dan Plante made it 2-0. "We got slapped in the face early, and it was good to react to it," MacTavish said later. "It was impressive how our

veterans led," said Richter. "Eight minutes into the game, we're down 2-0 and the place is rocking. I came to the bench to get water and those guys were saying, 'Keep it close and we'll be fine.'" Richter kept it close with a point-blank pad save on Ferraro. Then Kovalev got the Rangers rolling with a power play goal at 11:59, finishing a nice play by Larmer who kept the puck inside the zone and made a fine backhanded pass. They drew even on a second period power play goal, after Leetch intercepted a clearing pass and fed Zubov, whose hard slap shot wedged between the netting and the

goal's inside upright post. They took the lead when the Islander defense mishandled the puck and Messier trapped it, then swept in on a breakaway to score between Hextall's pads at 10:22. In the third, Larmer pounced on a Gilbert rebound to make it 4-2 at 8:34 and Messier added another breakaway goal at 17:08.

"Goaltending was probably the biggest factor," said Messier summing up the series, "but special teams were huge too. Our power play was lethal. But it wasn't easy. I've never played in a series that was easy, believe me."

Mark Messier and Ron Hextall after Game Four.

Game Four • April 24, 1994
Rangers 5, Islanders 2
FIRST PERIOD
1) NYI Thomas 1 (Krupp, Hogue) (PPG) 1:28
2) NYI Plante 1 (Turgeon, King) 7:24
3) NYR Kovalev 4 (Larmer, Zubov) (PPG) 11:59
PENALTIES – Anderson NYR (interference on the goaltender) 0:25; Plante NYI (charging) 2:21; Malakhov NYI (hooking) 10:21; Kypreos NYR (roughing), Thomas NYI (roughing) 18:02.
SECOND PERIOD
4) NYR Zubov 2 (Leetch) (PPG) 3:42
5) NYR Messier 3 10:22
PENALTIES – Kasparaitis NYI (roughing) 2:23; Hextall NYI (roughing - served by Acton) 3:42; Beukeboom NYR (cross-checking) 6:42; MacTavish NYR (roughing), Chynoweth NYI (roughing) 11:27.
THIRD PERIOD
6) NYR Larmer 2 (Nemchinov, Gilbert) 8:34
7) NYR Messier 4 (Beukeboom) 17:08
PENALTIES – Vaske NYI (cross-checking) 4:30; MacTavish NYR (cross-checking), Wells NYR (roughing), Vukota NYI (cross-checking, fighting major, game misconduct) 11:04.

Shots on goal	1	2	3	T
NY RANGERS	12	9	13	34
NY ISLANDERS	7	7	4	18

Goaltenders	TIME	SV	GA	ENG	DEC
NYR Richter	(60:00)	16	2	0	W
NYI Hextall	(60:00)	29	5	0	L

PP CONVERSIONS   NYR 2/6   NYI 1/2

Referee: Kerry Fraser.
Linesmen: Ray Scapinello, Ron Asselstine.
Attendance: 16,297.

MEETING FOR THE FOURTH TIME IN STANLEY CUP PLAY, the Rangers knocked out the Washington Capitals in five games, although the series was closer than the results indicated. Playing opportunistic hockey, the Rangers stayed in command most of the way against a determined Caps squad. The Rangers outscored the Caps 20-12 in the series, and 6-2 in third periods. Craig MacTavish's checking sparked the defensive effort, keeping Joe Juneau scoreless in all four Ranger wins.

By capturing Game Two, the Rangers won their sixth consecutive playoff game, breaking the club record of five set in 1940 and equalled in 1972. Two nights later, with their 3-0 win in Game 3, they extended the record to seven.

The Rangers penalty killing continued to excel, allowing only two goals – one of them scored on a five-on-three manpower advantage, in 25 Caps' power play opportunities. Brian Leetch and Mark Messier

recorded points in all five games, extending their point scoring streaks to nine games each. Leetch scored his fourth power play goal of the playoffs in Game Three, tying five other players for the club record for power play goals in one playoff year. In Game Five he recorded his 16th point, surpassing his own 1992 club record for points by a defenseman in one playoff year.

Mike Richter's shutout in Game Three was the fifth of his career, tying him with John Ross Roach for second place in club history, behind Davey Kerr who holds the Ranger postseason record with seven.

Craig MacTavish and Washington's Dale Hunter

GAME ONE
May 1, at Madison Square Garden
Rangers 6 • Capitals 3

SCRAPING THE RUST from the Rangers' seven-day layoff, Mark Messier came out flying, breaking in alone on Caps goalie Don Beaupre 16 seconds into the game. Beaupre made the save, but the Rangers grabbed an early lead for the fourth time in five games. Pinning the Caps in their own zone, Alexei Kovalev stopped Beaupre's clearing attempt along the boards and quickly threw it in front to Stephane Matteau, who redirected it behind Beaupre at 3:51. The Caps answered back 22 seconds later on Michal Pivonka's breakaway.

The Rangers gained a 2-1 lead as Craig MacTavish outhustled two Caps and fed Brian Noonan, standing alone in front of Beaupre. The goalie made the first stop but Noonan banged home the rebound at 16:28. The Caps tied it 2-2 on Kelly Miller's shot at 8:51 of the second. But when Kovalev forced a Caps player into taking a penalty just over three minutes later, the momentum swung back to the home team. On the power play, Sergei Zubov fired wide, but the puck caromed around the boards and he retrieved it at the left point and moved in toward the goal. He passed across to Brian Leetch on the right point and Leetch slapped a shot he later called a "knuckleball" that weaved through a screen and into the net at 12:47.

"The Leetch goal was very important to us," said Mike Keenan later. "We didn't come out strong. We seemed to be able to find the offense when we needed it and we're going to have to continue to capitalize when we have those opportunities." Three minutes after Leetch scored, MacTavish took a hit to move the puck to Noonan. Noonan spun away from Hatcher in the corner, skated unchecked out in front of the net and bounced a shot under Beaupre for his second goal of the game.

The Rangers made it 5-2 on their third straight goal when Greg Gilbert

banged a puck past Beaupre from the top of the crease at 3:06 of the third. Mike Ridley's backhander at 13:32 narrowed the margin, but Messier squelched the thought of a rally a minute later when he outraced John Slaney to a clearing shot by Joe Kocur and beat Beaupre at close range.

GAME TWO
May 3, at Madison Square Garden
Rangers 5 • Capitals 2

WASHINGTON ENTERED THE SERIES with some key injuries and got more bad news when goaltender Don Beaupre and center Michal Pivonka, the club's top playoff scorer, were unable to play Game Two. Rick Tabaracci took over for Beaupre and the banged-up Caps rose to the occasion, hustling and forechecking.

"An injured team is a dangerous team," Keenan said after the game. "They started really strong. They were emotionally very ready for the game." Richter made some big saves in the first five minutes, but a long shot by Hatcher slipped past him at 8:10. The Rangers tied the score at 16:42 when a shot by Alexander Karpovtsev off a pass from Sergei

Nemchinov was tipped in by Joe Kocur, who was screening Tabaracci.

Early in the second period Zubov stole the puck from a rushing Peter Bondra and quickly moved it ahead to Tikkanen. Once in the Caps zone, Tikkanen dropped a pass which Zubov fired past Tabaracci's glove at 1:38 for a 2-1 lead. Three minutes later, Ridley tied the score. Then midway through the period, Graves was dumped by Pat Peake and referee Kerry Fraser signaled a delayed penalty. Tikkanen replaced Richter as the extra attacker and drove down the left side to the net. From the right point, Messier tried to hit him with a pass but failed to click. Tikkanen grabbed the carom, fed Leetch at the left point and circled as the Rangers reloaded. Tikkanen again drove in from the left as Leetch passed across to Messier who again threw a cross ice pass down low. This

Esa Tikkanen came off the bench on a delayed penalty to score the winning goal in Game Two

GAME THREE
May 5, at US Air Arena
Rangers 3 • Capitals 0

PLAYING A NEAR-PERFECT GAME, the Rangers and Mike Richter registered their third shutout of the playoffs. In regular-season play, the club had also shut out the Caps in both games played in Landover. Once again, an early goal was the Rangers' best weapon. On a power play, Graves' backhander was stopped by Beaupre who was back in the Washington net. Leetch moved in picked up the rebound and fired a shot that hit Beaupre before glancing

time Tikkanen banged it home at 10:44.

The Caps pressed on a power play a few minutes later, but Richter flashed his glove to snag a slapper by Sylvain Cote. The Rangers broke the game open midway through the third when Steve Larmer, who was in forechecking, intercepted a pass and zipped it to Graves standing alone in the slot. He fired it home for a 4-2 lead at 10:47.

From the ensuing faceoff, Larmer hit Kovalev with a pass in the neutral zone. He fed a speeding Matteau, who tapped the puck in for the game's final goal. Despite the Rangers' three-goal margin, there was cause for concern as the Caps had numerous odd-man rushes and opportunities to capture

the game. "They outworked us tonight," Leetch told reporters, even though the Rangers outshot the Caps 25-24. "Winning makes you realize you're very fortunate and you've got to get your game back in gear."

Game Two • May 3, 1994
Rangers 5, Capitals 2

FIRST PERIOD
1) WSH Hatcher 2 (Ridley, Bondra) 8:10
2) NYR Kocur 1 (Karpovtsev, Nemchinov) 16:42
PENALTIES – Nemchinov NYR (interference) 3:03; Peake WSH (interference) 13:27.

SECOND PERIOD
3) NYR Zubov 3 (Noonan, Tikkanen) 1:38
4) WSH Ridley 4 (Poulin, Miller) 4:35
5) NYR Tikkanen 2 (Messier, Leetch) 10:44
PENALTIES – Messier NYR (cross-checking) 7:57; Konowalchuk WSH (roughing), Gilbert NYR (roughing) 11:39; Messier NYR (holding) 12:25; Ridley WSH (holding the stick) 15:01.

THIRD PERIOD
6) NYR Graves 4 (Larmer) 10:47
7) NYR Matteau 3 (Kovalev, Larmer) 11:06
PENALTIES – Woolley WSH (tripping) 1:46; Khristich WSH (interference) 12:38; Larmer NYR (tripping) 13:08; Ridley WSH (hooking), Karpovtsev NYR (slashing) 19:23; Krygier WSH (misconduct), Wells NYR (cross-checking) 20:00.

Shots on goal	1	2	3	T
WASHINGTON	9	8	7	24
NY RANGERS	6	12	7	25

Goaltenders	TIME	SV	GA	ENG	DEC
WSH Tabaracci	(60:00)	20	5	0	L
NYR Richter	(59:49)	22	2	0	W

PP Conversions WSH 0/4 NYR 0/4
Referee: Kerry Fraser.
Linesmen: Kevin Collins, Dan Schachte.
Attendance: 18,200.

off Cote's skate and into the net at 4:35.

Ten minutes later the Rangers again had the man advantage. Beaupre chased a shot by Leetch that had gone behind the net. Leetch followed the puck in and knocked it to Messier, who attempted a wrap-around into the empty net. The puck hit the near post and stayed out, but Messier got a second crack at it before Beaupre could get set again. The puck went in, giving the Rangers a 2-0 lead.

The Rangers made it 3-0 six minutes into the second when Jeff Beukeboom picked up a rebound in his own zone, skated to center and passed to Kovalev who crossed the Caps blue line and fed a cross ice pass to Larmer. Larmer snapped a high

Left: Let's just kiss and say goodbye: Esa Tikkanen gets in Keith Jones' face in Game Three.

Right: Despite this hit by Jay Wells, the Rangers had trouble controlling the Caps in Game Four.

shot behind Beaupre for the final goal of the game. Richter made a big pad save midway through the third period, robbing Dave Poulin on a shot from the slot and sealing the shutout.

"Our forwards and defensemen are giving them so little time, they have to set up quickly and get their shots away quickly," said Richter. Beukeboom called it "The best we've played in the playoffs. We came out very strong, limited their chances, converted our power plays, and killed penalties. Everyone was jumping, everything was working." Keenan called it "an excellent road game."

GAME FOUR
May 7 at US Air Arena
Capitals 4 • Rangers 2

WITH SEVEN BUSLOADS of cheering Ranger fans arriving early in Landover, it almost seemed like a home game during the pre-game warmup. The cheers continued when Graves batted home his own rebound 33 seconds into the game. The Rangers had another early lead but, facing elimination, Washington clawed back.

Around the seven-minute mark Todd Krygier broke through on a breakaway to tie the game. Late in the period, the Rangers failed to score

during a five-on-three power play. "That ignited their club," said Keenan, "They built a lot of momentum from that particular situation and, for the most part, outplayed us after that."

When the Caps enjoyed a five-on-three advantage of their own in the second period, Joe Juneau scored at 8:26. The Caps scored twice more before the period ended. Jason Woolley's shot found the net through a screen at 10:22 and Krygier scored on a rebound at 15:26.

Krygier's second goal was the Caps' 11th consecutive shot. The Rangers had yet to record a shot on goal in the second period. In an attempt to change the flow of the game, Keenan made a goaltending change, replacing Richter with Glenn Healy. The Rangers outshot the Caps 8-5 over the remainder of the period, but Beaupre's stretching glove save on Craig MacTavish with about a minute left kept the score at 3-1.

In the third, the Caps stressed defense and were outshot 10-0. During a five-minute power play, Noonan shoveled a loose puck into the net to close the gap, but this night belonged to Washington. The Rangers outshot the Caps 27-23 on the game.

The Rangers continued their trend of getting an early goal in Game Five when Graves deflected a shot into the net with less than two minutes gone in the first period.

Game Four • May 7, 1994
Capitals 4, Rangers 2

FIRST PERIOD
1) NYR Graves 5 (Messier) :33
2) WSH Krygier 1 (Cote) 7:26
PENALTIES – Kovalev NYR (holding) 4:51; Karpovtsev NYR (tripping) 9:47; Konowalchuk WSH (holding), Reekie WSH (cross-checking) 15:03.

SECOND PERIOD
3) WSH Juneau 4 (Hunter, Cote) (PPG) 8:26
4) WSH Woolley 1 (Hatcher, Juneau) 10:22
5) WSH Krygier 2 (Cote) 15:26
PENALTIES – Graves NYR (interference) :17; Noonan NYR (fighting major), Reekie WSH (fighting major) 4:45; Kovalev NYR (roughing) 6:40; Graves NYR (delay of game) 7:58; Larmer NYR (tripping) 11:02; Cote WSH (tripping) 13:19.

THIRD PERIOD
6) NYR Noonan 4 (Karpovtsev, Leetch) (PPG) 17:16
PENALTIES – Poulin WSH (hooking) 7:58; Poulin WSH (hitting from behind major, game misconduct) 14:07.

Shots on goal	1	2	3	T
NY RANGERS	9	8	10	27
WASHINGTON	7	16	0	23

Goaltenders	TIME	SV	GA	ENG	DEC
NYR Richter	(35:26)	16	4	0	L
NYR Healy	(24:34)	3	0	0	-
WSH Beaupre	(60:00)	25	2	0	W

PP Conversions   NYR 1/6   WSH 1/6
Referee: Paul Stewart.
Linesmen: Pat Dapuzzo, Randy Mitton.
Attendance: 18,130.

GAME FIVE
May 9, at Madison Square Garden
Rangers 4 • Capitals 3

THE MOST THRILLING GAME of the first two rounds featured a wide open first stanza. The Rangers scored early again. At 1:46, a shot from the point by Leetch hit Graves and went behind Beaupre. Four minutes later, with the Caps shorthanded, Hatcher's long clearing flip shot bounced strangely and eluded Richter who had come out of the net to play the hop. But the Rangers responded quickly, scoring twice while playing four-on-four.

Beukeboom pinched in at the blue line and knocked the puck to Messier along the right boards. He passed across to Leetch at the top of the left faceoff circle, and as Hatcher moved to stop him, Leetch slickly passed to Graves in the slot. Graves wristed the puck by Beaupre at 8:01. Fifty-five seconds later, Leetch's wrist shot was corralled by Tikkanen who had his back to Beaupre at the top of the crease. Tikkanen shoved a backhander between his own skates, under Beaupre, and into the goal.

Tabaracci replaced Beaupre and made several strong saves to keep the Caps alive. They drew closer when Shawn Anderson scored on a rebound at 16:20 and the game remained 3-2 through a defensive, scoreless second period. Cote's slap shot at the start of the third evened the score.

With under four minutes remaining in regulation time, Zubov gloved Hatcher's clearing attempt and held it briefly as Leetch moved into the left faceoff circle. Leetch took Zubov's pass, skated into the slot, and walked in on Tabaracci untouched, shooting the puck between his pads for the series-clinching goal.

The Caps had one last gasp in the final seconds, but with players piled in front of him, Richter came up with several big saves. The Rangers outshot the Caps 36-31. "We're proud of beating the Capitals and we have a lot of respect for them," said Graves after the game, "but basically we have a couple of steps left and the next one will be the toughest of the first three." He was right.

Right: Kevin Lowe battles Dale Hunter. Below: Brian Leetch scored the game-winning goal on a feed from Sergei Zubov.

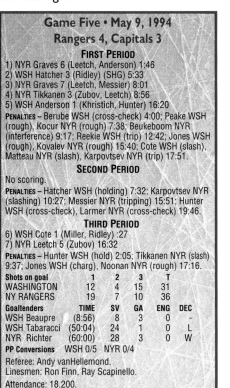

Game Five • May 9, 1994
Rangers 4, Capitals 3

FIRST PERIOD
1) NYR Graves 6 (Leetch, Anderson) 1:46
2) WSH Hatcher 3 (Ridley) (SHG) 5:33
3) NYR Graves 7 (Leetch, Messier) 8:01
4) NYR Tikkanen 3 (Zubov, Leetch) 8:56
5) WSH Anderson 1 (Khristich, Hunter) 16:20
PENALTIES – Berube WSH (cross-check) 4:00; Peake WSH (rough), Kocur NYR (rough) 7:38; Beukeboom NYR (interference) 9:17; Reekie WSH (trip) 12:42; Jones WSH (rough), Kovalev NYR (rough) 15:40; Cote WSH (slash), Matteau NYR (slash), Karpovtsev NYR (trip) 17:51.

SECOND PERIOD
No scoring.
PENALTIES – Hatcher WSH (holding) 7:32; Karpovtsev NYR (slashing) 10:27; Messier NYR (tripping) 15:51; Hunter WSH (cross-check), Larmer NYR (cross-check) 19:46.

THIRD PERIOD
6) WSH Cote 1 (Miller, Ridley) :27
7) NYR Leetch 5 (Zubov) 16:32
PENALTIES – Hunter WSH (hold) 2:05; Tikkanen NYR (slash) 9:37; Jones WSH (charg), Noonan NYR (rough) 17:16.

Shots on goal	1	2	3	T
WASHINGTON	12	4	15	31
NY RANGERS	19	7	10	36

Goaltenders	TIME	SV	GA	ENG	DEC
WSH Beaupre	(8:56)	8	3	0	-
WSH Tabaracci	(50:04)	24	1	0	L
NYR Richter	(60:00)	28	3	0	W

PP Conversions WSH 0/5 NYR 0/4

Referee: Andy vanHellemond.
Linesmen: Ron Finn, Ray Scapinello.
Attendance: 18,200.

IN A SERIES THAT WILL BE DISCUSSED and remembered for years to come as the best New York has ever seen, the Rangers and Devils battled toe-to-toe through seven games (and then some) of twists and turns, ups and downs, and highs and lows. Finally, in the third double-overtime game of the series, Stephane Matteau scored to propel the Rangers into the Stanley Cup Finals.

For the Rangers, it was the first time in club history they had won a Game Seven in overtime. For Matteau, it was his second overtime goal against the Devils. Only two other Rangers had scored two OT goals in a single series: Don Raleigh against Detroit in the 1950 Finals and Pete Stemkowski against Chicago in the 1971 Semi-Finals.

Mike Richter won his 12th playoff game, surpassing John Davidson's club record of 11 wins by a goalie in one playoff season. His shutout in Game Two left him alone in second place on the Rangers' all-time list for playoff shutouts. It was his fourth shutout of the 1994 playoffs, making him the seventh goaltender to own a share of the NHL record for most shutouts in a single playoff year. He was the second Ranger to equal this mark, joining Davey Kerr who had four playoff shutouts in 1937. Richter was seven seconds away from his fifth shutout when the Devils scored in Game Seven.

Mark Messier's hat trick in Game Six staved off elimination for the Rangers and was the tenth three-goal performance in club history.

GAME ONE
May 15, at Madison Square Garden
Devils 4 • Rangers 3 (2 OT)

ONCE AGAIN, THE RANGERS OPENED a series following a long layoff and began with an early goal. After advancing the puck to Mark Messier, Sergei Zubov received a drop pass in return before blasting a shot that beat Martin Brodeur at 3:39. The Rangers proceeded to storm the Devils net and Brodeur looked shaky, especially when Alexei Kovalev hit the goalpost on a breakaway. Brodeur then settled down and, in what would prove to be a pattern of play in regulation time during the series, the Devils tied the score when John MacLean circled the net and threw the puck in front where it hit a Ranger skate and went in behind Mike Richter at 18:16.

Hard work by Greg Gilbert in the corner resulted in a pass to Sergei Nemchinov whose high one-timer

---

Martin Brodeur's performance in goal for the Devils in Game One was a prelude to his strong play throughout the series.

Game One • May 15, 1994
Devils 4, Rangers 3 (2 OT)
FIRST PERIOD
1) NYR Zubov 4 (Messier) 3:39
2) NJ MacLean 6 (Albelin, Driver) 18:16
PENALTIES – None.
SECOND PERIOD
3) NYR Nemchinov 1 (Gilbert, Noonan) 17:50
PENALTIES – Nicholls NJ (hooking) 2:36; Fetisov NJ (holding) 5:08; Richer NJ (roughing), Lowe NYR (roughing) 7:58; Tikkanen NYR (holding) 12:45.
THIRD PERIOD
4) NJ Guerin 1 (Nicholls) 5:50
5) NYR Larmer 4 (Messier) (PPG) 11:05
6) NJ Lemieux 6 (MacLean, Nicholls) 19:17
PENALTIES – Dowd NJ (interference) 10:52; Lowe NYR (cross-checking) 12:08; Stevens NJ (roughing), MacTavish NYR (highsticking) 15:36.
FIRST OVERTIME PERIOD
No scoring.
PENALTIES – Fetisov NJ (roughing), Richer NJ (roughing), Noonan NYR (roughing), Tikkanen NYR (roughing) 4:58.
SECOND OVERTIME PERIOD
7) NJ Richer 6 (Carpenter) 15:23
PENALTIES – Richer NJ (roughing), Lemieux NJ (unsportsmanlike conduct), Beukeboom NYR (roughing), Tikkanen NYR (unsportsmanlike conduct) 4:14.

Shots	1	2	3	10T	20T	T
NJ	8	7	13	11	9	48
NYR	8	10	8	9	3	38

Goaltenders	TIME	SV	GA	ENG	DEC
NJ Brodeur	(95:08)	45	3	0	W
NYR Richter	(95:23)	34	4	0	L

PP Conversions NJ 0/2 NYR 1/3
Referee: Bill McCreary.
Linesmen: Gord Broseker, Randy Mitton.
Attendance: 18,200.

beat Brodeur with 2:10 remaining in the second period and put the Rangers back in the lead. But 5:50 into the third, Bill Guerin tied the score again. The Rangers went up 3-2 midway through the period on hard work by Steve Larmer. He dug the puck out of the corner, passed to Messier for a shot and got Messier's rebound on his backhand, whipping the puck into the open net at 11:05.

The Devils had trouble mounting an effective attack until Brodeur was replaced by an extra attacker in the last minute of regulation time. The Devils then stormed the Ranger net. After Richter stopped consecutive close in chances, Claude Lemieux banged the puck home with 43 seconds left on the clock.

The Devils had a new life and began to play with great confidence in overtime. Both teams had excellent chances thwarted by the goalies and Kovalev again hit the goal post in the second OT stanza. With less than five minutes left in the second overtime period, Stephane Richer took a pass from Bob Carpenter, skated past Adam Graves and fired a wrist shot that Richter got his stick on but could not stop. The Devils had a 4-3 overtime victory. "We weren't as sharp as we wanted to be," said Messier, "We've been through plenty of adversity this season. I'm not doubting how we'll respond."

Stephane Richer was thwarted by The Rangers defense on this play, but later scored the winning goal in double overtime in Game One.

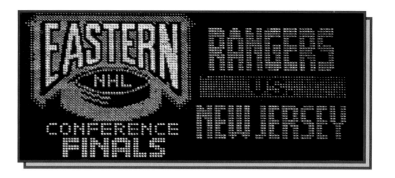

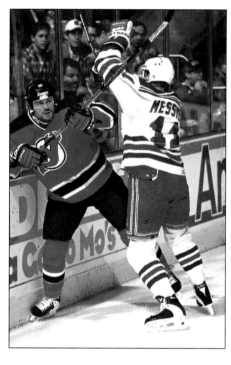

Mark Messier landed solid hits on Scott Stevens (above) and Ken Daneyko (right) before scoring a goal on his first shift of Game Two.

GAME TWO
May 17 at Madison Square Garden
Rangers 4 • Devils 0

THE RANGERS RESPONDED to the Devils' challenge with one of their strongest performances to date. Messier banged Scott Stevens behind the New Jersey net, then hit Ken Daneyko. Glenn Anderson and Esa Tikkanen teamed up to crunch Lemieux and the puck squirted free. Messier picked it up behind the net and stuffed it behind Brodeur just 1:13 into the game. "Mess took the game into his hands," said Graves. "He took control right from the drop of the puck in a manner only a guy like him can do. That's why he's Mark Messier."

The Rangers continued to play the body, with great open-ice hits by Messier, Kevin Lowe, and Jay Wells creating Ranger chances. Brodeur was especially sharp as the period closed. In the second, the Devils picked up the tempo. Richter's best and, perhaps, most memorable save of the

Below: Mike Richter's great save on Bill Guerin prevented the Devils from tying the score in the second period.

series, was on Bill Guerin near the 13 minute mark. Guerin went wide around Leetch down the left wing before sharply cutting in front of the goal. Richter stayed with him as he crossed the crease and, as Guerin shot, stuck out his catching glove, bobbling the puck before trapping it.

Shortly thereafter, the Devils had a five-on-three advantage for 1:25 and Richter had to make several good saves to keep the score 1-0. Early in the third period, the Rangers broke into the Devils zone. Esa Tikkanen was hooked to the ice and slid into Brodeur, moving him from the goal. Nemchinov fired a loose puck into the open net, giving the Rangers some breathing room. Just past the six minute mark, Glenn Anderson, who had not scored in 10 games, broke in on Brodeur and deked him before shooting the puck into the empty net.

The Rangers final tally at 8:38 was a beauty. Messier kept the puck in at the blue line as Leetch took off toward the net. Messier's soft pass hit Leetch perfectly and he moved into the slot where he dished off to Graves on the other side of the slot for a one-timer that no goalie could stop.

EASTERN
NHL
CONFERENCE
FINALS

RANGERS
vs
NEW JERSEY

GAME THREE

May 19 at Meadowlands Arena
Rangers 3 • Devils 2 (2 OT)

IN A GAME AS EXCITING as it was long, the Rangers provided yet another early thrill when Messier attracted double coverage as he stepped over the blue line and hit Graves with a pass. Graves moved in and blasted the puck past Brodeur at 2:43. The Devils tied the score three minutes later when the rebound off a shot by Viacheslav Fetisov hit MacTavish and bounced into the net.

In the second period, Larmer and Valeri Zelepukin traded power play goals. Zelepukin's was the Devils' first power play goal of the series. Through 40 minutes the Rangers dominated play, outshooting the Devils 32-15. The third period and the first overtime were scoreless with chances evenly divided between the two teams. The game turned nasty at points, most notably when Bernie Nicholls crosschecked Kovalev while the officials were occupied breaking up a skirmish between Graves and Lemieux.

The goaltenders traded enormous saves in regulation time and in the OT. Richter made a superb split save on Stephane Richer with five minutes remaining in the third period. In extra time, Richter stopped MacLean early, Brodeur caught Zubov's wrister and blocked Lowe's dangerous short shot. Richter stopped Nicholls on his doorstep. Fetisov knocked away Nemchinov's attempt at an open net.

Richter made back-to-back big stops on Tommy Albelin in double overtime

Game Three • May 19, 1994
Rangers 3, Devils 2 (2OT)

FIRST PERIOD
1) NYR Graves 9 (Messier, Beukeboom) 2:43
2) NJ Fetisov 1 (McKay, Holik) 5:38
PENALTIES – Niedermayer NJ (holding) 7:13; Anderson NYR (interference) 10:13; Lemieux NJ (cross-checking) 14:42; Tikkanen NYR (roughing), Zelepukin NJ (roughing) 17:27.

SECOND PERIOD
3) NYR Larmer 5 (Leetch, Graves) (PPG) 9:35
4) NJ Zelepukin 3 (Driver, Richer) (PPG) 15:50
PENALTIES – Karpovtsev NYR (holding) 2:38; MacLean NJ (cross-checking) 4:28; Kovalev NYR (highsticking) 6:45; Guerin NJ (cross-checking) 8:44; Messier NYR (highsticking), Daneyko NJ (roughing) 11:28; Stevens NJ (roughing) 12:15; Larmer NYR (interference on the goaltender) 14:17; Wells NYR (elbowing) 17:58.

THIRD PERIOD
No scoring.
PENALTIES – Guerin NJ (boarding) 1:05; Messier NYR (hooking) 2:24; Beukeboom NYR (roughing), Carpenter NJ (roughing) 7:06; MacTavish NYR (interference on the goaltender) 11:11.

FIRST OVERTIME PERIOD
No scoring.
PENALTIES – Anderson NYR (roughing), Albelin NJ (cross-checking) 6:52; Matteau NYR (roughing), Guerin NJ (roughing) 16:54.

SECOND OVERTIME PERIOD
5) NYR Matteau 4 6:13
PENALTIES – None.

Shots	1	2	3	1OT	2OT	T
NYR	15	17	7	9	2	50
NJ	7	8	7	6	3	31

Goaltenders	TIME	SV	GA	ENG	DEC
NYR Richter	(86:13)	29	2	0	W
NJ Brodeur	(86:13)	47	3	0	L

PP Conversions NYR 1/6 NJ 1/7
Referee: Terry Gregson.
Linesmen: Swede Knox, Ray Scapinello.
Attendance: 19,040.

Brodeur later halted Graves on a break-in try.

At 3:30 of the second overtime period, Lemieux and Albelin broke in on a two-on-one. Richter slid out to stop Albelin's shot and, while lying on his back, was able to get his right pad on the rebound. Three minutes later, with the Rangers pressing around the Devils goal, Anderson dug the puck out from behind the net to Kovalev, whose shot was stopped. Matteau whacked home the rebound and set off a wild Rangers celebration. "The puck came across the crease two or three times," said an exhilarated Matteau. "I just saw it at the last second. I just put my stick down and saw the puck at my feet. Growing up in Quebec, you dream about scoring a goal in the Stanley Cup finals. Tonight it happened." He was one round shy of fulfilling his boyhood dream, but no one was complaining.

Above: Martin Brodeur pokechecks Sergei Nemchinov in overtime action.

Below: The Rangers were pressing when the winning goal was scored by Stephane Matteau on this backhander from a scramble in front.

GAME FOUR
May 21 at Meadowlands Arena
Devils 3 • Rangers 1

ALTHOUGH THE **NHL SUSPENDED** Bernie Nicholls for one game as a result of his crosscheck to Kovalev, the Devils came out strong, scoring the opening goal for the first time in the series when Stephane Richer connected on a power play wraparound at 10:17. New Jersey added another on Guerin's breakaway at 16:54. Richter was then replaced by Glenn Healy and various Rangers found their ice time curtailed as Keenan tried to shake the team up.

The Rangers worked their way back to 2-1 on a power play goal when Larmer fed Messier behind the net and he passed to Matteau for a one-timer right in front at 8:47 of the second. The Devils continued to play stingy defensive hockey and wait for errors. They got the break they were waiting for in the third when Healy and Karpovtsev miscommunicated behind the net and Zelepukin wrapped the puck around the left post into the empty cage.

All four Devils lines contributed effective checking which limited the Rangers ability to move the puck. Brodeur stopped almost everything the defense did not. The Rangers, who had 50 shots on goal in Game Three, were held to just 22 shots on the Devils net.

In an attempt to reverse the momentum in Game Four, Ranger coach Mike Keenan replaced starting goaltender Mike Richter with Glenn Healy following the Devils' second goal late in the first period.

Game Four • May 21, 1994
Devils 3, Rangers 1
FIRST PERIOD
1) NJ Richer 7 (Dowd, MacLean) (PPG) 10:17
2) NJ Guerin 2 (Stevens) 16:54
PENALTIES – Leetch NYR (hooking) 10:01; Beukeboom NYR (fighting major), Peluso NJ (fighting major) 15:22; Lowe NYR (tripping) 17:51.

SECOND PERIOD
3) NYR Matteau 5 (Messier, Larmer) (PPG) 8:47
PENALTIES – Fetisov NJ (roughing) 4:15; Zelepukin NJ (tripping) 8:19; Lowe NYR (tripping) 12:12; Daneyko NJ (holding) 16:16.

THIRD PERIOD
4) NJ Zelepukin 4 13:18
PENALTIES – Guerin NJ (highsticking) 3:16; Lowe NYR (holding) 9:29.

Shots on goal	1	2	3	T
NY RANGERS	3	12	7	22
NEW JERSEY	11	8	6	25

Goaltenders	TIME	SV	GA	ENG	DEC
NYR Richter	(16:54)	9	2	0	L
NYR Healy	(43:06)	13	1	0	-
NJ Brodeur	(60:00)	21	1	0	W

PP Conversions NYR 1/4 NJ 1/4
Referee: Dan Marouelli.
Linesmen: Swede Knox, Ray Scapinello.
Attendance: 19,040.

GAME FIVE
May 23 at Madison Square Garden
Devils 4 • Rangers 1

ALTHOUGH suffering injuries to key players, the Rangers started strongly. MacTavish barely missed an opportunity for a backhander into an empty net in the first five minutes, but the puck slid off his stick. New Jersey was then penalized, but it was the Devils and not the Rangers who capitalized when Lemieux broke in for a shot which Richter stopped. Nicholls escaped from the checking of Kovalev and batted in the rebound at 6:49.

Playing with the lead, the Devils again began to limit the Rangers' chances. Early in the third period, Karpovtsev attempted to bat a bouncing puck behind the net, but instead he directed it on goal, where Richter dove for it as it squirted along the goal line. Mike Peluso nudged it across for a 2-0 lead, silencing the noisy Garden. The Devils scored twice more with Nicholls and Chorske getting the goals before Tikkanen's slap shot squeaked through Brodeur's pads for the only Ranger goal at 16:33. Each team finished the game with 26 shots.

"In the playoffs, inevitably, there's always the ultimate test," MacTavish said after his team was pushed to the brink of elimination. "You either respond to it or you go home. This is what the playoffs are all about, challenges and conquests, and you have to respond."

Bernie Nicholls scored twice for the Devils in Game Five.

GAME SIX

May 25 at Meadowlands Arena
Rangers 4 • Devils 2

WITH THE RANGERS FACING ELIMINATION, the drama of the moment was heightened when Mark Messier "guaranteed" victory at practice the day before. Additionally, the NHL suspended Jeff Beukeboom for the game because of a hit from behind on Stephane Richer in Game Five. Doug Lidster replaced him and Ed Olczyk replaced Brian Noonan who was injured. For both players it would be their first playoff action.

When the puck dropped, it was the Devils who dictated play, getting two first-period goals. Scott Niedermayer's centering pass was deflected behind Richter by Nemchinov at 8:03 and Lemieux deflected home a shot by Niedermayer at 17:32. The Rangers would continue to struggle until late in the second period, but Richter was formidable in keeping the Rangers in the game, stopping numerous odd-man rushes.

Near the six minute mark of the second, Keenan called a timeout and juggled his lines and defense pairings. With Kovalev now on Messier's right wing, the Rangers attempted to pick up the pace. As the period neared its end, Messier passed to Kovalev, who was able to get some extra skating room in the Devils zone. He faked a slapshot, moved in closer and ripped a 30-footer past Brodeur at 18:19. The Rangers had new life.

Immediately pressing their advantage, the Rangers began to move the puck with renewed confidence as the Devils backpedaled. Early in the third, Kovalev entered the Devils zone and passed to Messier who was speeding toward the Devils goal. His backhander between Brodeur's skate and the post tied the game at 2:48. Nine minutes later, with the Rangers still pressing and playing four-on-four,

Game Six • May 25, 1994
Rangers 4, Devils 2

FIRST PERIOD
1) NJ Niedermayer 2 8:03
2) NJ Lemieux 7 (Niedermayer, Nicholls) 17:32
PENALTIES – Larmer NYR (roughing) 9:15; Holik NJ (hooking) 15:12; Driver NJ (highsticking) 19:07.

SECOND PERIOD
3) NYR Kovalev 5 (Messier) 18:19
PENALTIES – Messier NYR (unsportsmanlike conduct), Nicholls NJ (unsportsmanlike conduct) 14:07; Tikkanen NYR (tripping) 18:51.

THIRD PERIOD
4) NYR Messier 8 (Kovalev, Leetch) 2:48
5) NYR Messier 9 (Kovalev, Leetch) 12:12
6) NYR Messier 10 (SHG) 18:15
PENALTIES – Tikkanen NYR (roughing), Niedermayer NJ (roughing) 11:32; Anderson NYR (slashing) 17:11; Anderson NYR (unsportsmanlike conduct, misconduct), Stevens NJ (misconduct), Nicholls NJ (highsticking, roughing, misconduct) 19:40; Gilbert NYR (slashing), Daneyko NJ (slashing) 19:43.

Shots on goal	1	2	3	T
NY RANGERS	9	13	14	36
NEW JERSEY	13	13	4	30

Goaltenders	TIME	SV	GA	ENG	DEC
NYR Richter	(60:00)	28	2	0	W
NJ Brodeur	(58:40)	32	3	1	L

PP Conversions NYR 0/3 NJ 0/3
Referee: Kerry Fraser.
Linesmen: Pat Dapuzzo, Gerard Gauthier.
Attendance: 19,040.

Defenseman Doug Lidster was effective playing in Game Six, his first game of the 1994 playoffs.

Mark Messier's performance in Game Six ranks with the finest in Stanley Cup history. With the Rangers trailing 2-0, he set up Alexei Kovalev for a second-period goal and then scored the game-tying and game-winning goals in the third period. He added an empty netter to complete his hat trick and force Game Seven.

shot that bounced once and slid into the vacant net. His third goal of the period sealed the victory.

"I played against Mark for nine years," said Jay Wells, "and nothing scared me more than when he got that real serious look of determination in his eye. In the third period, he had that." The captain said, "No one man wins a hockey game. Mike Richter was incredible. Everyone played well." The Rangers outshot the Devils 14-4 in the third period and 36-30 in the game.

Leetch weaved laterally through center, gained the zone and passed to Kovalev, who blasted a shot that Brodeur was able to knock down. Messier, bursting through the backchecking of Nicholls, batted the rebound into the net at 12:12 and the Rangers had a lead for the first time since Matteau's overtime winner in Game Three.

In the final two minutes, the Devils went on the power play and pulled Brodeur to create a six-on-four advantage, but the puck came to Messier directly from a faceoff. Without looking, he fired a 175-foot

EASTERN
NHL
CONFERENCE
FINALS

RANGERS
vs
NEW JERSEY

GAME SEVEN

May 27 at Madison Square Garden
Rangers 2 • Devils 1 (2 OT)

THIS MEMORABLE SERIES could not end with any more drama than that offered by Game Seven. With Beukeboom and Noonan returning to the lineup, the Rangers dominated the early going, but Brodeur kept the game scoreless. In the second period, it was Richter's turn to shine, making a skate save on Bobby Holik's close-in shot and a glove save on MacLean's wrister. Midway through the period, Messier won a faceoff, pulling the puck back to Graves who passed to Leetch along the left boards. Leetch moved to cut in behind the net but, with his path blocked by Guerin, he pivoted away and spun in front of the goal. He then

shoved a backhander through three players and between Brodeur's skate and the left goal post to give the Rangers a 1-0 lead.

The Devils quickly pressed to tie, but Richter stopped Lemieux, Nicholls, and Guerin before the period ended. Brodeur was equally sharp keeping the game close, stopping Nemchinov's attempted redirection early in the third. Although their lead was slim, the Rangers seemed in command, even after icing the puck a few times in the last minute of regulation time with Brodeur out of the net for an extra attacker.

With less than 20 seconds remaining in regulation time, Richter attempted to move the puck after making a save, but referee Bill

McCreary whistled the play dead, causing a faceoff to Richter's right. With the Garden fans already in joyous celebration, the Devils got the puck down low to Lemieux, who fed it across the crease to Zelepukin who shot and then shoved the rebound under Richter's outstretched pad to tie the game with 7.7 seconds remaining on the clock.

The Garden crowd was dumbstruck. A sense of foreboding lasted through the intermission and resurfaced in the overtime whenever fortunes seemed to favor the Devils. Although it was the Rangers who dominated play, with Brodeur forced to make a total of 19 saves, the fans uttered a collective shriek at every Devils advance.

Mike Richter made big stops on the Devils' less frequent but no less dangerous rushes, including turning aside a bullet drive by Stephane Richer seconds before the game finally ended. The finale occurred early in the second overtime period when Matteau beat Niedermayer in a race for the puck along the left boards, skated behind the net and attempted to wrap the puck around the right post. The puck hit Brodeur's stick and slid over the line, ending the game at 24:24 of overtime and sending the fans into a frenzy. The chant "We want the Cup!" erupted throughout the Garden. The Rangers outshot the Devils 48-32 in this NHL playoff classic.

"We still have seven games or less to go in our season," said Matteau, again the OT hero. "We won one trophy tonight, but I want to see the other one here."

"That right there was the greatest hockey series I've ever played in my life," said Tikkanen, who had played in a few. "It was amazing, it was incredible, it was awesome."

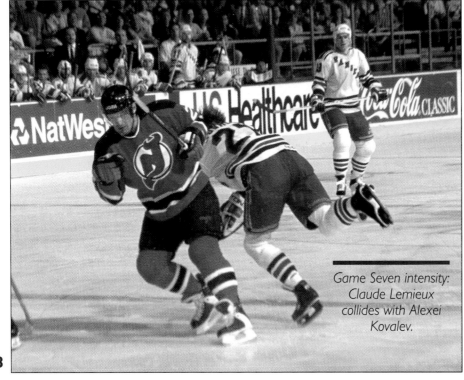

Game Seven intensity: Claude Lemieux collides with Alexei Kovalev.

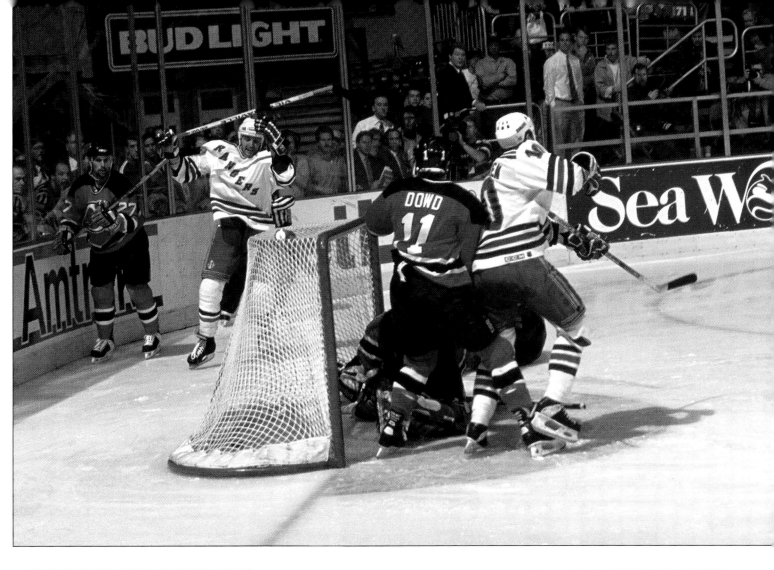

Game Seven • May 27, 1994
Rangers 2, Devils 1 (2OT)

FIRST PERIOD

No scoring
PENALTIES – None.

SECOND PERIOD

1) NYR Leetch 6 (Graves, Messier) 9:31
PENALTIES – Lemieux NJ (interference) 12:13.

THIRD PERIOD

2) NJ Zelepukin 5 (Lemieux, Richer) 19:52
PENALTIES – Kovalev NYR (elbowing) 6:32.

FIRST OVERTIME PERIOD

No scoring
PENALTIES – None.

SECOND OVERTIME PERIOD

3) NYR Matteau 6 4:24
PENALTIES – None.

Shots	1	2	3	1OT	2OT	T
NJ	10	5	9	7	1	32
NYR	11	11	6	15	5	48

Goaltenders	TIME	SV	GA	ENG	DEC
NJ Brodeur	(83:23)	46	2	0	L
NYR Richter	(84:24)	31	1	0	W

PP Conversions   NJ 0/1   NYR 0/1

Referee: Bill McCreary.
Linesmen: Kevin Collins, Ray Scapinello.
Attendance: 18,200.

Above: Stephane Matteau's second double-overtime goal of the series clinched Game Seven.

Right: Ranger coaches, trainers, and players, including the "Black Aces" who did not dress for Game Seven, share the moment of victory. Several of the club's reserves attempted to invoke the Ranger goal in overtime by wearing inside-out "rally jackets."

NEW YORK RANGERS / VANCOUVER CANUCKS
STANLEY CUP CHAMPIONSHIP

FOR THE FIRST TIME SINCE 1979, the Rangers advanced to the Stanley Cup Finals. Like the Rangers, the Vancouver Canucks, had made significant personnel changes at the trade deadline and were a much different team than the one that started the season in October. Seeded seventh in the Western Conference, the Canucks were underdogs in successive series against Calgary, Dallas and Toronto. Trailing Calgary three games to one in the first round of the playoffs, the Canucks rode superb goaltending by Kirk McLean to three consecutive overtime wins to clinch the series. The Canucks were clearly on a roll and appeared to gain confidence with each game. They needed just five games to eliminate the Stars and Maple Leafs, earning their first berth in the Finals since 1982. Heading into Game One of the Finals, the Canucks had been idle for seven days.

The Rangers, meanwhile, were coming off an exhilarating but draining series against New Jersey.

Game One • May 31, 1994
Canucks 3, Rangers 2 (OT)

FIRST PERIOD
1) NYR Larmer 6 (Kovalev, Leetch) 3:32
Penalties - Wells NYR (cross-checking) 1:47; Linden VAN (tripping) 2:27; McIntyre VAN (roughing), Lowe NYR (roughing) 8:50; Craven VAN (slashing) 10:35; Beukeboom NYR (interference) 15:54.

SECOND PERIOD
No scoring.
Penalties - Messier NYR (hooking) :20; Lidster NYR (tripping) 8:49; Courtnall VAN (interference) 13:18; Momesso VAN (interference on the goaltender) 16:15; Beukeboom NYR (highsticking) 19:34.

THIRD PERIOD
2) VAN Hedican 1 (Adams, Lumme) 5:45
3) NYR Kovalev 6 (Leetch, Zubov) 8:29
4) VAN Gelinas 5 (Ronning, Momesso) 19:00
Penalties - None.

OVERTIME
5) VAN Adams 6 (Ronning, Bure) 19:26
Penalties - Momesso VAN (roughing), Gilbert NYR (roughing) 9:31.

Shots on goal	1	2	3	1OT	T
VANCOUVER	10	5	7	9	31
NY RANGERS	15	9	13	17	54

Goaltenders	TIME	SV	GA	ENG	DEC
VAN McLean	(79:26)	52	2	0	W
NYR Richter	(79:26)	28	3	0	L

PP Conversions   VAN 0/5   NYR 0/4

Referee: Terry Gregson.
Linesmen: Randy Mitton, Ray Scapinello.
Attendance: 18,200.

Despite being outplayed in overtime, the Canucks won Game One on Greg Adams' one-timer.

The Canucks featured the most exciting player in the National Hockey League, 23 year-old Pavel Bure, nicknamed "The Russian Rocket." He began the Finals with 13 playoff goals, tops in the League, and had recorded a point in 15 consecutive playoff games. Stopping Bure was a hot topic among the New York fans and the media in the three days leading up to the series.

GAME ONE

May 31 at Madison Square Garden
Canucks 3 • Rangers 2 (OT)

ANYONE PREDICTING that the Rangers would suffer an emotional let-down following their dramatic series with the Devils had yet to grasp the businesslike character of the club. Just the opposite occurred in Game One as the home team again opened with a flourish, buzzing around the Vancouver zone and firing pucks at Kirk McLean as Vancouver struggled to keep pace.

For the 11th time in 16 playoff games, the Rangers opened the scoring in the first six minutes. Playing four skaters a side due to offsetting minor penalties, Brian Leetch dropped a pass to Alexei Kovalev on the back end of a give-and-go. Kovalev cruised down the slot, deked David Babych and took a wrist shot from 20 feet out that was stopped by McLean. The rebound came to Steve Larmer, who fired a shot that hit the right post, bounced off McLean's right pad and settled into the net at 3:32.

The Rangers continued to press through the first period and into the second, skating well and passing crisply, taking advantage of the Canucks' sluggishness. But McLean came up with big saves time and again. Pavel Bure was effectively checked most of the game, as the Rangers did not back away and allow him skating room, instead challenging him and stripping him of the puck. When the Rangers took penalties, they pressured Vancouver's power play unit and rendered the Canucks ineffective, drawing appreciative cheers from the fans.

Early in the third period, killing a penalty, Messier broke in alone and tried go between McLean's legs, but the Vancouver netminder shut the door. Adam Graves, trailing for the rebound, couldn't get a good shot at the bouncing puck. Nearing the six minute mark of the third, Vancouver defenseman Jyrki Lumme got the puck from Greg Adams deep in the attacking zone as a delayed penalty was being called on the Rangers. He walked out of the corner and took a sharp angle shot that Richter stopped and directed up the slot. Lumme's defense partner, Bret Hedican, moved in from the blue line and fired the puck home to tie the game at 5:45.

The Rangers came right back when Leetch, taking the puck that Zubov had fired off the glass in the neutral zone, penetrated Vancouver territory and drew the attention of the Canucks' checkers. This allowed Kovalev to steam down the left side and when Leetch slammed a hard pass down low, Kovalev was alone in front to one-time it into the net for a 2-1 lead. The Rangers again attacked after the goal, but McLean would not allow his team to be put away. As the period neared its conclusion, a shot by Cliff Ronning was deflected on its way to the goal by Martin Gelinas. Richter appeared to trap the puck between his arm and his body, but it dropped behind him and slid into the net at 19:00. It was the second consecutive game in which a last-minute goal sent the Rangers into overtime.

In overtime, the Rangers continued to attack, outshooting

GAME TWO
June 2 at Madison Square Garden
Rangers 3 • Canucks 1

RECOGNIZING THAT VANCOUVER had grown stronger as Game One wore on, the Rangers began Game Two with their trademark offensive flurry in the first few minutes and, again, were rewarded with the first goal of the game. This time it came from an unexpected source, former Canuck Doug Lidster. The veteran defenseman, who had been inserted into the lineup for Game Six of the Devils series, had continued his strong play and was rewarded by Mike Keenan with increased ice time. With Kevin Lowe replaced in the lineup by Alexander Karpovtsev because of recurring shoulder problems, Lidster epitomized the Rangers depth on defense.

The goal resulted from Lidster's decision to grab a loose puck and skate down the left boards with just over six minutes into the game. He cut sharply to the net and slid by Gerald Diduck on the inside until he was right in front of McLean. The Canucks' goalie stopped Lidster's short side attempt, but as Lidster shot again, Diduck pushed the Ranger, and Lidster knocked McLean and the puck over the goal line at 6:22.

Now in the lead, the Rangers poured it on, trying to go up by two, but reminiscent of Game One, McLean kept his team alive. At 14:04 of the first period the Canucks tied the score. Cliff Ronning, who created opportunities for his team throughout the game, shot the puck high on Richter's short side. It disappeared into the Ranger goalie's sweater, then dropped behind him into the crease. Sergio Momesso pounced on the puck and shoveled it home. Given new life, the Canucks began to dominate play

Doug Lidster's drive to the net resulted in the Rangers' first goal in Game Two.

Vancouver by a wide margin but McLean continued to play strongly. He made stops on Graves, Tikkanen, Larmer, Zubov, Kovalev, Leetch, and the hero of other Ranger overtimes, Stephane Matteau. In the last minute of the first overtime period, with the Rangers applying considerable pressure, Leetch rifled a shot that beat McLean but hit the crossbar and ricocheted out past the faceoff dot. Beukeboom moved in to corral the rebound but Bure reached it first. He chipped the puck out of the zone to speedy Cliff Ronning, who gained the blue line but was angled to the boards by Tikkanen. Ronning threw a centering pass to Greg Adams who was flying unchecked toward the net.

He one-timed a shot past Richter's glove hand to win the game for Vancouver.

Kirk McLean's 52 saves were the most ever recorded by a goaltender in a Stanley Cup Final game decided in the first overtime period. "Vancouver walked out of here with a win tonight because of their goaltender. They were very fortunate," Mike Keenan said after the game. "It's not like we haven't been here before," said Matteau. "We had the same exact situation in the last series. We have to forget about this like we did against New Jersey. We came back then, we can come back now."

as the period closed and Richter had to be sharp on a chance by Bure in the last minute.

The Canucks and Rangers played an even second period as each team had good chances on power plays, including one in which Ronning hit the crossbar. Midway through regulation time, Graves was called for tripping and the Rangers set out to force the Canucks with aggressive penalty killing. Glenn Anderson forced a hurried pass by Trevor Linden "He was passing to the far point," Anderson later recalled, "I think it was for Lumme, and Mark stepped up into the play and got himself a partial breakaway."

Messier pushed the puck ahead in an attempt to outrace Vancouver defenseman Jeff Brown. "McLean came out to poke check the puck and got a piece of it, but it hit Mark's pants and was trickling in behind the net. I tried to force my way up into the play and avoid Lumme's back-checking," Anderson continued. "I just went to the net as hard as I could. Mess fed it

out to me and I had an empty net." Alone in front, Anderson scored the go-ahead goal as the Garden crowd erupted.

Along with the lead, the Rangers grabbed the game's momentum and, led by Leetch, continued to outplay Vancouver, generating solid scoring opportunities. Shots rang off the posts or crossbar, trickled wide, or otherwise went unconverted. Richter, too, got help from the posts but also made strong saves on Momesso and Craven.

As regulation time ticked down, and the Canucks pulled McLean for the extra attacker, Richter prevented another last-minute disaster for the Rangers. With about ten seconds left to play, a pass from Brown found

Martin Gelinas standing alone on one side of the crease. Gelinas' first shot was stopped by a kick of Richter's right leg and his second went under Richter's thigh, but his goal stick was there to knock it away. Leetch then picked up the puck, and lofted a long backhand shot that traveled the length of the ice into the Canuck net to clinch the game.

The Rangers again shut down Bure, whose point-scoring streak was stopped at 16, two games short of the NHL record. "That was definitely a big game, no question," said Messier. "But now the next one is the biggest game of the year. Again."

Mark Messier's shorthanded breakaway resulted in this short pass to Glenn Anderson. Anderson's goal put the Rangers ahead to stay.

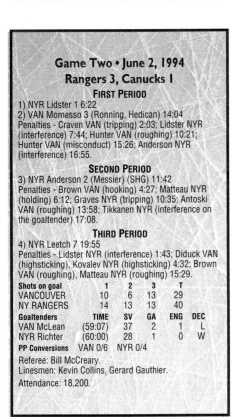

Game Two • June 2, 1994
Rangers 3, Canucks 1
FIRST PERIOD
1) NYR Lidster 1 6:22
2) VAN Momesso 3 (Ronning, Hedican) 14:04
Penalties - Craven VAN (tripping) 2:03; Lidster NYR (interference) 7:44; Hunter VAN (roughing) 10:21; Hunter VAN (misconduct) 15:26; Anderson NYR (interference) 16:55.
SECOND PERIOD
3) NYR Anderson 2 (Messier) (SHG) 11:42
Penalties - Brown VAN (hooking) 4:27; Matteau NYR (holding) 6:12; Graves NYR (tripping) 10:35; Antoski VAN (roughing) 13:58; Tikkanen NYR (interference on the goaltender) 17:08.
THIRD PERIOD
4) NYR Leetch 7 19:55
Penalties - Lidster NYR (interference) 1:43; Diduck VAN (highsticking), Kovalev NYR (highsticking) 4:32; Brown VAN (roughing), Matteau NYR (roughing) 15:29.

Shots on goal	1	2	3	T
VANCOUVER	10	6	13	29
NY RANGERS	14	13	13	40

Goaltenders	TIME	SV	GA	ENG	DEC
VAN McLean	(59:07)	37	2	1	L
NYR Richter	(60:00)	28	1	0	W

PP Conversions   VAN 0/6   NYR 0/4

Referee: Bill McCreary.
Linesmen: Kevin Collins, Gerard Gauthier.
Attendance: 18,200.

GAME THREE

June 4 at Pacific Coliseum
Rangers 5 • Canucks 1

THE FINALS MOVED to a city awash in Stanley Cup fever, with fans cheering for the Canucks' first-ever Stanley Cup Finals win on home ice. Lowe returned to the line-up wearing oversized shoulder pads, but Karpovtsev was not scratched as Zubov was sidelined with a chest injury. The Rangers had the game's first good scoring chance after only thirty seconds of play when Leetch zig-zagged past Dave Babych only to be stopped in front by McLean. Less than a minute later, Pavel Bure broke in on Richter, after quick relays from Lumme, Adams and Linden. When Bure tucked the puck between Richter's feet, the fans leaped to their feet in celebration of a 1-0 Vancouver lead.

Bure continued to fly, drawing Jay Wells into a tripping penalty on his next shift. But the Rangers penalty killers remained nearly impenetrable and Richter did the rest. Midway through the period, Adam Graves' hard work drew Lumme into a holding penalty and swung the momentum over to the Rangers. The Canucks killed the penalty to Lumme, but New York began to move the puck well.

The Rangers got their first big break of the series when Leetch flipped the puck toward the goal from the left point. McLean went down on one knee to steer it to the corner but did so a split-second too late. The puck bounced off the underside of his stick glove and slid through his legs into the net to tie the game at 13:39, and the fans grew quiet. At 15:40, Lumme drew MacTavish into a holding penalty but led by Lidster's shot blocking, the Rangers again killed it off. As the

---

Pavel Bure's high stick on Jay Wells was the turning point in Game Three as the Canucks never recovered after their star player was assessed a game misconduct.

Game Three • June 4, 1994
Rangers 5, Canucks 1

FIRST PERIOD
1) VAN Bure 14 (Linden, Adams) 1:03
2) NYR Leetch 8 13:39
3) NYR Anderson 3 (Nemchinov, Beukeboom) 19:19
Penalties - Wells NYR (tripping) 2:54; Anderson NYR (roughing), Hunter VAN (charging) 5:42; Lumme VAN (holding) 9:57; MacTavish NYR (holding) 15:40; Leetch NYR (tripping) 17:56; Lowe NYR (highsticking), Messier NYR (roughing), Ronning VAN (highsticking), Momesso VAN (roughing) 18:12; Bure VAN (highsticking major, game misconduct) 18:21.

SECOND PERIOD
4) NYR Leetch 9 (Tikkanen, Beukeboom) 18:32
Penalties - Lowe NYR (roughing) 5:34; Messier NYR (roughing), Antoski VAN (roughing) 16:28.

THIRD PERIOD
5) NYR Larmer 7 :25
6) NYR Kovalev 7 (Graves, Messier) (PPG) 13:03
Penalties - Tikkanen NYR (hooking) 3:13; Hedican VAN (holding) 5:34; McIntyre VAN (holding) 7:58; MacTavish NYR (holding) 9:46; Momesso VAN (cross-checking) 11:42; Gelinas VAN (roughing) 16:35; Antoski VAN (cross-checking, roughing) 19:19.

Shots on goal	1	2	3	T
NY RANGERS	9	10	6	25
VANCOUVER	11	5	9	25

Goaltenders	TIME	SV	GA	ENG	DEC
NYR Richter	(60:00)	24	1	0	W
VAN McLean	(60:00)	20	5	0	L

PP Conversions NYR 1/7 VAN 0/6
Referee: Andy vanHellemond.
Linesmen: Ray Scapinello, Randy Mitton.
Attendance: 16,150.

period ended, play grew chippy, resulting in a flurry of penalties.

After a faceoff, Bure high-sticked Jay Wells, cutting him and breaking his nose. Referee Andy vanHellemond issued the Canucks star a high-sticking major and a game misconduct at 18:21 of the first period. "It certainly took a player out of their line-up who we had to be aware of every time he's on the ice," said Leetch later. "It didn't affect our overall game plan, but I'm sure that it took a little bit away from them. He's a game breaker and to have him off really helped." Stunned, the Canucks and their fans went flat and the Rangers capitalized. Playing four-on-four, Beukeboom passed ahead to Nemchinov in the neutral zone. Nemchinov tipped the puck into the Vancouver zone and chased in after it. He beat Glynn to the puck along the right boards, then spun away and moved unchecked laterally into the high slot. Glenn Anderson, meanwhile, had joined the play and headed to the net. When Nemchinov shot, Anderson, with his back to the goal, deflected the puck past McLean for an all-important late goal and a 2-1 lead at 19:19.

In the second, ill-will simmered between players on both teams. Vancouver's only good scoring chance came on a hard shot by Ronning that was ticketed for the lower left corner before being gloved by Richter in full stretch. The Rangers dominated play. Playing four-on-four with under two minutes to go in the period, Beukeboom passed ahead to Leetch who touch-passed the puck to Tikkanen at center-ice. Tikkanen carried the puck in as Leetch sped toward the goal. Tikkanen fired and McLean made the stop, but the rebound came right to Leetch who picked it up and roofed a backhander past McLean to make it 3-1.

Twenty-five seconds into the third, Larmer's dump-in pinballed off of John McIntyre and Babych, sliding into the goal before McLean could react. "We got some good bounces tonight and that hasn't happened in an awful long time," said Larmer. "Working hard makes those breaks happen and we worked hard for 60 minutes tonight." All that remained was for the Rangers to score their first powerplay goal since Game Four of the Devils series. It came off of a beautiful series of fakes by Kovalev after a breakaway pass from Graves. Kovalev's short wrist shot beat McLean at 13:03. Though the Rangers controlled play, each team had 25 shots on goal.

Glenn Anderson celebrates what proved to be the game-winning goal in Game Three.

Kovalev's seventh playoff goal finished the scoring. The puck can be seen high in the back of the net.

GAME FOUR
June 7 at Pacific Coliseum
Rangers 4 • Canucks 2

IT WAS A GAME THE RANGERS
WANTED to win. It was a game
the Canucks had to win. The
Rangers had Sergei Zubov back in
the lineup, but Vancouver had the
better of the play in a thrilling first
period during which the 0-for-17
Canuck power play began to click.
On a holding penalty to Adam
Graves, Vancouver captain Trevor
Linden scooped up a deflected pass
in the slot and shot through a tangle
of players at 13:25 for his first goal
of the series.

The Ranger penalty killers were
tested again a minute later, when
Messier slammed Momesso and was
assessed a boarding major. Aggressive
penalty killing forced Linden into a
penalty for holding a Ranger player's
stick, nullifying the advantage at 15:07.
The Rangers' four-on-four play
thoughtout the playoffs had been
outstanding, as they had outscored
their opponents 7-2. This time,
however, they were victimized when
Bure broke down the right side, cut
sharply around Zubov and in toward
Richter. The goalie poked the puck
away, but Ronning was unchecked and
picked up the puck and fired it home

at 16:19 for a 2-0 lead. The Canucks
regained the man advantage shortly
thereafter, but again squandered the
chance when Courtnall was called for
tripping Tikkanen.

As it turned out, the Rangers
were actually shorthanded for less
than 90 seconds during Messier's
major. The Canucks' inability to
capitalize during the major helped
shift the momentum in the second
period, as did the efforts of Mike
Keenan.

"We could easily have said after
the first period that it might not
happen tonight," said Beukeboom.
"We've got to give credit to Mike
Keenan, who came in and said we're

not done yet." Around the four-
minute mark, the Rangers broke out
three-on-two. Greg Gilbert fed
MacTavish at center and, as
MacTavish carried the puck in,
Leetch jumped up into the play.
MacTavish dropped a pass to Leetch
and as he shot, Joe Kocur, checked
by Tim Hunter, drove to the net.
Leetch's shot went in and the
Rangers had new life at 4:03.
Vancouver stormed back and, in one
flurry, fired six shots at Richter in
fifteen seconds. The goalie kept his
balance and stopped each one. As
the game opened up, McLean made
a big glove save on Larmer. Bure
then sped through center ice, broke
through Leetch and Beukeboom and
headed into the Rangers zone.
Leetch tripped Bure when he
reached with his stick in an attempt
to stop the speedy winger. Referee
Terry Gregson immediately signaled
for a penalty shot at 6:31.

Bure's penalty shot was the
decisive moment of the game. As
Bure moved in on Richter, the

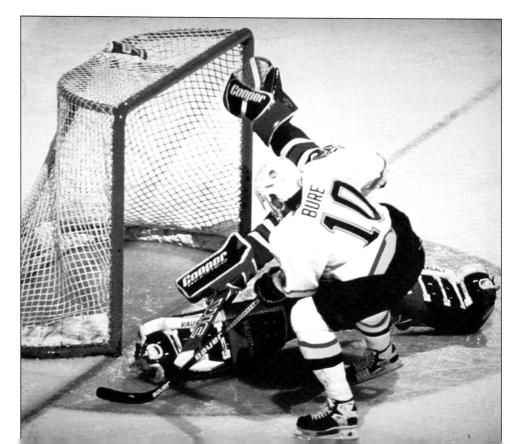

*The turning point of Game Four was
Mike Richter's acrobatic save on Pavel
Bure's penalty shot. A goal by Bure
would have given the Canucks a 3-1
lead in the second period.*

goalie moved out to cut off the net, then backed in as Bure got closer. Inside of ten feet, Bure faked to his right and went left. Richter wasn't fooled. He kept his feet and then flashed out his right leg, doing the splits to stop Bure right in front. "It was a classic confrontation between one of the most, if not *the* most, electrifying forward in the NHL and one of the outstanding goaltenders in the League," said Keenan. "It was the most important save of Michael's career. It gave us a chance to come back."

And come back they did. On a power play, Zubov faked once then slapped the puck through Graves' screen, tying the game at 19:44. The Rangers were called for too many men on the ice early in the third period, but when Larmer stepped between Lumme and Brown to steal the puck behind the Canucks net, Lumme held him and nullified the advantage.

Richter made a big stop on Hedican during the four-on-four.

Steve Larmer killed penalties and buzzed around the Canucks zone all night. Vancouver's Jyrki Lumme drew a penalty on this play,

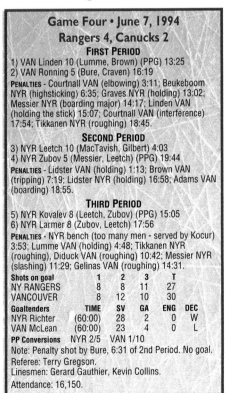

During a later four-on-three situation, the Rangers' penalty killing prevented even a single shot by the Canucks. Richter then made another series of stops on Linden and Brown. In command everywhere but on the scoreboard, the Rangers took charge after Gelinas wrestled Lowe to the ice and was called for holding. Zubov passed to Leetch deep in his own end, and Leetch moved out of his zone through center. Just before the Vancouver blue line, he faked left then veered right, stepping around Glynn and steaming deep into Canucks territory. Kovalev flew into the lane that Leetch had vacated and, when Leetch reached the low slot, he pushed the puck ahead to Kovalev who one-timed it high into the net for a 3-2 lead at 15:05.

The Rangers added a final goal three minutes later, when Babych kicked at Larmer's long flip shot, only to see the puck change direction and fly past a stunned McLean, who appeared to have lost his concentration and did not move. The Rangers were one win away from a Stanley Cup championship.

GAME FIVE
June 9 at Madison Square Garden
Canucks 6 • Rangers 3

ON A NIGHT ABOUNDING WITH ANTICIPATION, in which New York could witness a Rangers Stanley Cup triumph, the early breaks in Game Five favored the Canucks. A Ranger power play generated little as it was Richter who was called upon to make the toughest save of the two minutes. Shortly after the teams returned to even strength, Zubov barely missed cashing in a Kovalev rebound that dropped from Kirk McLean's glove. McLean also stopped Leetch's big shot from the point. At the other end of the ice, Richter got his toe on a shot by Linden around the eight-minute mark.

Midway through the period, Esa Tikkanen's blast from the blueline flew behind McLean into the Vancouver net, but the goal was disallowed because offside had been called. TV replays revealed that Tikkanen appeared to have been onside on the play. After the play was whistled down, Momesso slashed Leetch along the boards and other players piled in. When order was restored, penalties were assessed and the Rangers lost Jeff Beukeboom, who received an instigator penalty and was ejected from the game.

About four minutes later, Leetch passed in the slot to Graves whose shot beat McLean but hit the crossbar. Killing a penalty in the first minute of the second period, Graves stole the puck from Jeff Brown and broke in alone on McLean who made the stop. Richter then returned the favor, stopping Brown's hard slapper. Messier, Noonan, and Leetch all had

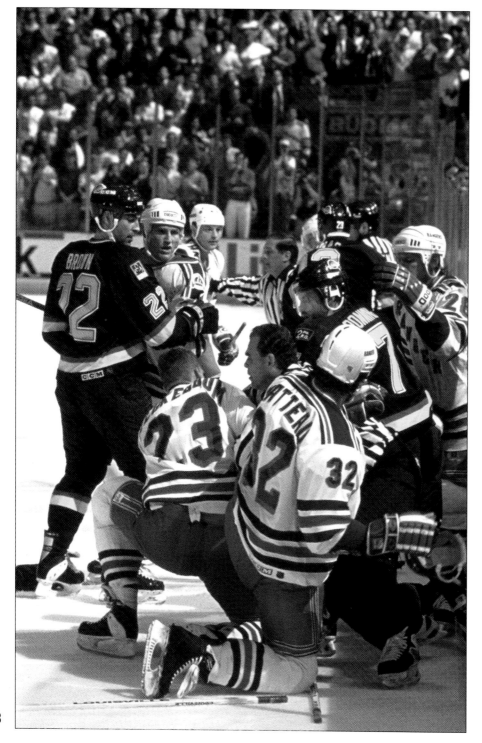

Jeff Beukeboom (23) was ejected from Game Five after this first period skirmish.

good chances early in the period, but when Ronning attracted double coverage rushing into the Rangers zone, he passed smartly behind his back to Brown who was open on his right. Brown's shot beat Richter's glove hand to give Vancouver a 1-0 lead at 8:10.

Two minutes later, Courtnall received an elbowing major for flattening Zubov, but the Rangers could do little with the resulting five-minute advantage. The fans tried to rally the Rangers at the start of the third period, but 26 seconds in, Courtnall buried a rebound from a shot by Nathan Lafayette to make it 2-0.

Just over two minutes later, Bure's shot was stopped by Richter, but the rebound hit Leetch's leg and bounced into the net at 2:48. Trailing 3-0, the Rangers were forced to take chances and open up offensively. First Kovalev passed from the corner to Lidster who took a long shot from the point. Screened by Steve Larmer, the puck

floated past McLean at 3:27. The Rangers were on the board.

About three minutes later, Matteau centered the puck to Larmer. While Nemchinov was being wrestled to the ice by Brown in front of the Vancouver net, Larmer found an opening and put the puck there. The crowd, now invigorated, chanted, "We Want The Cup!" And three minutes later, Graves passed through center to Anderson who delivered a slick behind-the-back pass to Messier along the right boards. Messier drove to the net and put a wrist shot knee high to the stick side of McLean, tying the game as the Garden exploded at 9:02.

"The gambling paid off," Mike Keenan said later, "but then it didn't." Immediately after the faceoff, the Rangers tried to attack once more. But the Canucks gained possession and Pavel Bure crossed the Ranger blue line on a three-on-two rush. He passed to Dave Babych and the veteran defenseman, who had deflected a puck into his own net in each of the previous two games, beat

Richter low to the short side to restore Vancouver's lead.

The Rangers continued to press. Nemchinov broke in on McLean and got off a backhander, but the Canucks goalie trapped it in his midsection. Soon after, Geoff Courtnall converted a rebound of Lafayette's shot at 12:20, and Bure knocked in Ronning's rebound 44 seconds later. Eight goals had been scored in the third period, tying the Stanley Cup Finals record for most goals by both teams in one period. The Canucks' five third-period goals tied the record for most goals by one team in one period in the Finals.

After the final buzzer, Messier told reporters. "This game is over with right now. We don't have time to sit back thinking about this game. We had some breakdowns tonight. We need to start thinking about Game Six."

The Garden fans were certainly thinking about Game Six as well. As the clock wound down, with their club losing by three, they chanted, "Let's Go Rangers."

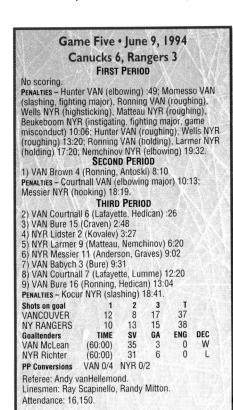

Game Five • June 9, 1994
Canucks 6, Rangers 3
FIRST PERIOD
No scoring.
PENALTIES – Hunter VAN (elbowing) :49; Momesso VAN (slashing, fighting major), Ronning VAN (roughing), Wells NYR (highsticking), Matteau NYR (roughing), Beukeboom NYR (instigating, fighting major, game misconduct) 10:06; Hunter VAN (roughing), Wells NYR (roughing) 13:20; Ronning VAN (holding), Larmer NYR (holding) 17:20; Nemchinov NYR (elbowing) 19:32.
SECOND PERIOD
1) VAN Brown 4 (Ronning, Antoski) 8:10
PENALTIES – Courtnall VAN (elbowing major) 10:13; Messier NYR (hooking) 18:19.
THIRD PERIOD
2) VAN Courtnall 6 (Lafayette, Hedican) :26
3) VAN Bure 15 (Craven) 2:48
4) NYR Lidster 2 (Kovalev) 3:27
5) NYR Larmer 9 (Matteau, Nemchinov) 6:20
6) NYR Messier 11 (Anderson, Graves) 9:02
7) VAN Babych 3 (Bure) 9:31
8) VAN Courtnall 7 (Lafayette, Lumme) 12:20
9) VAN Bure 16 (Ronning, Hedican) 13:04
PENALTIES – Kocur NYR (slashing) 18:41.

Shots on goal	1	2	3	T		
VANCOUVER	12	8	17	37		
NY RANGERS	10	13	15	38		
Goaltenders	TIME	SV	GA	ENG	DEC	
VAN McLean	(60:00)	35	3	0	W	
NYR Richter	(60:00)	31	6	0	L	

PP Conversions   VAN 0/4   NYR 0/2
Referee: Andy vanHellemond.
Linesmen: Ray Scapinello, Randy Mitton.
Attendance: 16,150.

Mike Richter faced 37 shots in the highest scoring game of the Finals. This low drive hit the outside of the net.

NEW YORK RANGERS VANCOUVER CANUCKS
STANLEY CUP CHAMPIONSHIP

GAME SIX
June 11 at Pacific Coliseum
Canucks 4 • Rangers 1

ON THE LATEST CALENDER DATE in Stanley Cup history, the Rangers again attempted to close out Vancouver. The Canucks still searched for their first final series victory in front of their white-shirted, towel-waving fans. Two minutes in, Bure attempted to set the tone with a hard check on Leetch. Soon after, Beukeboom took the game's first penalty when he was called for elbowing.

The Rangers, who had killed all but one of the 31 Canuck power plays in the first five games of the series, killed this one as well with help from Richter, who made big saves during one wild scramble. Richter continued to hold the fort and on a delayed penalty, made his ninth save of the period, diving to his right to deny Gelinas. With Leetch whistled off for interference, Linden won the faceoff from Tikkanen and got the puck back to Brown, whose point shot deflected off Tikkanen and sailed over Richter's right shoulder at 9:42, just three seconds after the penalty had been called.

The Canucks pressed for more, but Richter continued to keep the Rangers in the game, making a big glove save on Linden and stopping Bure on the short-side and on a breakaway. The Canucks outshot the Rangers 15-6 over the first 15 minutes and Richter was all that stood in their way. He kept it up in the second, kicking out his leg to stop Adams on a point-blank shot a minute in. With Momesso in the box shortly after, Bure stole the puck, broke in and slapped a wicked shot that bounced off Richter's facemask, deflecting above the net. Richter was unhurt on the play.

The Rangers began to generate more offense in the second and around 11 minutes in, Noonan set up Anderson whose shot hit the crossbar. The Rangers kept pressuring as Larmer broke in on a two-on-one with Zubov and McLean slid to stop his shot with a leg save. Lumme picked up the puck, got it quickly to Bure who fed Courtnall on a two-on-one back the other way. Courtnall cut in front and took a backhander, but he didn't get all of the puck. It hit Lidster's stick before drifting under Richter and over the goal line for a 2-0 lead at 12:29.

Just over two minutes later on a power play, Messier, Leetch, and Kovalev passed the puck along the right side until Kovalev shook free for a shot that hit Craven and was

Alexei Kovalev scored the only Ranger goal in Game Six.

redirected past McLean. The Rangers were on the board at 14:42. They were dominating play as well, having outshot the Canucks 11-6 to this point in the period. Before the second period ended, Bure cut sharply around Lowe and was in alone on Richter who made another spectacular stop on the Russian Rocket.

The Rangers began the third period with sustained pressure but, at 8:35, Jeff Brown fired from the top of the right circle through a partial screen, beating Richter to his stick side to give the Canucks a 3-1 lead. Two minutes later, Bure beat Lowe, broke in and released a dangerous backhander but Richter made another acrobatic glove save. In the closing minutes, Adams hit Courtnall with a pass deep in the

Rangers zone. He deked Richter to the ice and put a backhander into the net at 18:28. The puck bounced out quickly and play continued with the officials believing the puck hit the crossbar. The Rangers carried the puck into the Vancouver zone and, 34 seconds later, Messier jammed it past McLean. After a video review, Courtnall's goal was awarded and Messier's nullified.

With Vancouver's win, the Rangers' commanding lead in the series had evaporated. The club's supporters were downcast and nervous but the players appeared unruffled. "Before the season, if you had said we'd be going home with a chance to win the Stanley Cup in Game Seven, we'd be pretty happy with that," said Messier after the game. "We don't have any reason to hang our heads or be disappointed or ashamed. What this is, is an opportunity to go home and win the Stanley Cup."

Facing elimination, the Canucks played their best game of the series in Game Six, pursuing the Rangers all over the ice. Here Vancouver captain Trevor Linden attempts to tie up Esa Tikkanen behind goaltender Kirk McLean.

NEW YORK RANGERS **VANCOUVER CANUCKS**
STANLEY CUP CHAMPIONSHIP

GAME SEVEN
June 14 at Madison Square Garden
Rangers 3 • Canucks 2

IT WAS THE TENTH GAME SEVEN in Stanley Cup Finals history, and the first series to go the distance since 1987. Six Rangers played in that 1987 game and their coach was behind one of the benches. At Monday's practice, Mike Keenan had passionately addressed the players, emphasizing that victory in Game Seven would unite the club forever. Messier would later call it the most powerful speech he'd heard in his years in hockey. "He seized the moment. He took control. We were definitely floundering and the guys were looking for leadership. Mike came through when we needed it the most," said the Ranger captain.

On game night, the tense atmosphere in the Garden differed from the party-like feeling surrounding Game Five. The Rangers made one lineup change: Nick Kypreos was dressed in place of the injured Joe Kocur.

The game started slowly, but by the middle of the first period, the Rangers began to pick up the pace. Leetch fought off a pair of Canuck forecheckers and slipped a pass to Messier on his right. Messier chipped the puck off the boards, eluding Pavel Bure. He picked it up himself and brought the puck down the right side into the Vancouver

Brian Leetch opened the scoring with this wrist shot just beyond the reach of goaltender Kirk McLean.

zone. Messier then circled counter-clockwise away from the net, drawing two checkers with him. He fed a pass to Zubov, who had stepped into the lane Messier had vacated. Zubov skated freely toward the net and McLean came out to cut down the angle, but Zubov spied Leetch, who had moved into the left faceoff circle, and threw him a pass. Leetch was at a sharp angle, but McLean, who had lost his balance and was unable to get back into position, couldn't lunge fast enough as Leetch's shot from the lower edge of the circle bulged the twine at 11:02 for a 1-0 Rangers lead. Leetch's goal, his eleventh of the post-season, left him only one shy of the NHL record for most goals by a defenseman in one playoff year.

After the goal, the Rangers forecheckers went to work, the MacTavish-Noonan-Tikkanen line playing effectively down low, drawing Lumme into a cross-checking infraction. On the ensuing power play, Zubov rushed the puck through center and advanced it between Craven and Brown as they converged on him. Kovalev picked up the puck in the left circle and slipped a pass to Graves, who was skating alone in the slot. His 15-footer beat McLean low to the stick side at 14:45 and the Rangers led 2-0. It was Graves' first goal in ten games.

Vancouver applied pressure as the period waned. Bure circled into the slot for a shot that Richter stopped, and the rebound came to Craven at the right of the net. With Beukeboom defending the goal, Craven pushed the puck under him, but it rolled through the crease inches from the goal line before the Rangers cleared it to safety.

Early in the second period, Beukeboom collided with Antoski along the boards. Once again, Beukeboom would be lost for the night, not because of a penalty but because of a knee injury.

The Rangers controlled play early in the period. Brown took an interference penalty at 4:38. During the power play, the Rangers were called for a delayed penalty and McLean left the net for an extra attacker. Linden took a pass from Bure, put his shoulder down to fend off Leetch, moved the puck from forehand to backhand and flipped it past Richter at 5:21 to narrow the margin.

Later in the period, with Babych off for tripping, Noonan cut through the slot with the puck and a scramble developed. McLean stopped Noonan and Graves poked at the rebound before it came to Messier at the side of the net. He jabbed at it and, as John McIntyre tried to smother puck, it caromed off McIntyre's leg and into the net for a 3-1 lead at 13:29.

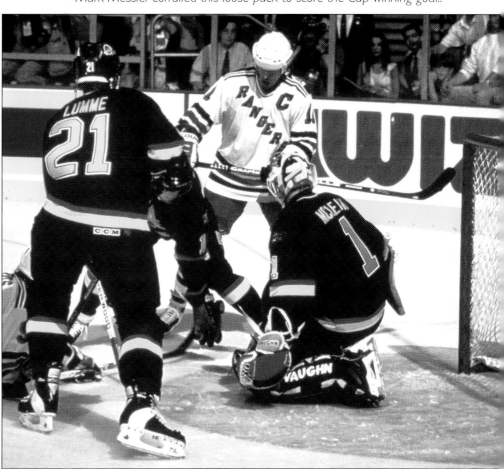

Mark Messier corralled this loose puck to score the Cup-winning goal..

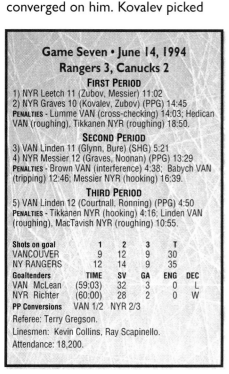

Game Seven • June 14, 1994
Rangers 3, Canucks 2
FIRST PERIOD
1) NYR Leetch 11 (Zubov, Messier) 11:02
2) NYR Graves 10 (Kovalev, Zubov) (PPG) 14:45
PENALTIES - Lumme VAN (cross-checking) 14:03; Hedican VAN (roughing), Tikkanen NYR (roughing) 18:50.
SECOND PERIOD
3) VAN Linden 11 (Glynn, Bure) (SHG) 5:21
4) NYR Messier 12 (Graves, Noonan) (PPG) 13:29
PENALTIES - Brown VAN (interference) 4:38; Babych VAN (tripping) 12:46; Messier NYR (hooking) 16:39.
THIRD PERIOD
5) VAN Linden 12 (Courtnall, Ronning) (PPG) 4:50
PENALTIES - Tikkanen NYR (hooking) 4:16; Linden VAN (roughing), MacTavish NYR (roughing) 10:55.

Shots on goal	1	2	3	T
VANCOUVER	9	12	9	30
NY RANGERS	12	14	9	35

Goaltenders	TIME	SV	GA	ENG	DEC
VAN McLean	(59:03)	32	3	0	L
NYR Richter	(60:00)	28	2	0	W

PP Conversions   VAN 1/2   NYR 2/3
Referee: Terry Gregson.
Linesmen: Kevin Collins, Ray Scapinello.
Attendance: 18,200.

NEW YORK RANGERS VANCOUVER CANUCKS

STANLEY CUP CHAMPIONSHIP

With a two-goal lead restored, Richter stopped Gerald Diduck and then foiled Ronning, stacking his pads on the rebound. A late-period penalty to Messier was killed so effectively that the Canucks could not gain the zone and set up.

Determined not to fall into a defensive shell, the Rangers came out strong for the third period. Just past the four-minute mark, Tikkanen lost the puck to Bure and was forced to take a penalty for hauling down the Russian Rocket. Ronning, Brown, and Courtnall passed smartly and Linden finished the play at 4:50 to make the score 3-2.

Vancouver pressed, looking for the tying goal. Richter stopped Lafayette's close-in attempt as the Rangers began to slow the pace of the game with determined defensive play. Larmer and MacTavish were particularly effective. Larmer turned defense to offense with two good mid-period scoring chances, one of which hit the post, while MacTavish won key face-offs and took Linden off the ice with coincidental minors.

With the minutes ticking down, Vancouver turned up the heat again as Zubov stopped Bure one-on-one and Richter kicked out a shot by Brown. With less than seven minutes left, Ronning passed to Gelinas, whose shot at the wide-open net grazed the post as Richter dove to his left. With six minutes remaining, Lafayette's one-timer forced Richter into a full stretch,

and again the puck clanged off the post. But the Rangers defense held, forcing the play out of danger time and time again.

The crowd roared at PA announcer Bob Galerstein's call of "Last minute of play in the period." McLean sprinted to the bench for an extra attacker. A succession of icing calls, reminiscent of past playoff games in which the Rangers eventually surrendered a late tying goal, left the crowd uneasy.

With only a few seconds remaining, the Rangers cleared the puck, and believing time had expired, began to celebrate with players leaping high in the air despite the fact that icing had been called.

MacTavish and Bure took the game's final faceoff in the circle to Richter's right with 1.6 seconds showing on the clock. Linesman Ray Scapinello dropped the puck and MacTavish drew it back to the end boards as the horn sounded, fireworks exploded, and the Rangers were 1994 Stanley Cup champions.

Two trophy presentations took place at center ice. Brian Leetch, who led all scorers in the 1994 playoffs with 34 points, was named winner of the Conn Smythe Trophy as playoff MVP. Mark Messier became the first Ranger captain to hoist the Stanley Cup in triumph at Madison Square Garden.

The dream realized. The Stanley Cup champion New York Rangers savor the moment after a 3-2 win over the Canucks in Game Seven.

Thank you from the New York Rangers

·

1994 Stanley Cup Champions